European Classics
for Women

Absolute
Monologues

European Classics
for Women

EDITED BY ALISON REID
AND SIMON READE

ABSOLUTE  CLASSICS

Reprinted in 1997 by Oberon Books Limited, incorporating
Absolute Classics, 521 Caledonian Road, London, N7 9RH.
Tel: 0171 607 3637 / Fax: 0171 607 3629

First published in 1994 by Absolute Press

Cover and text design: Ian Middleton

Computer output and copy editing: Andrew McLeish

Printed by Arrowhead Books Ltd, Reading

ISBN 0 948230 73 8

Contents

Preface

I

In only five years, the independent Absolute Classics has published over seventy plays from the European classic repertoire. Most of these plays-in-translation have received important productions on the modern stage. Seen in the playhouses of the Royal Shakespeare Company and the Royal National Theatre, throughout the world with Cheek by Jowl and other touring companies, in the intimacy of that room above a London pub – the Gate Theatre, Notting Hill – the plays have attracted widespread critical acclaim and popularity amongst theatre-goers. They are all translated and adapted by Britain's leading dramatists, giving a dynamic contemporary voice to classic theatre.

Absolute Classics pioneer the rediscovered, the British première; thus the plays hold an extra fascination. A collection of monologues is a treasure-trove of the European repertoire, from the Greeks to the 20th Century. Monologues are touchstones. They inspire you to explore the complete play from where each character comes.

The monologues selected here are presented in a rough historical order, period by period, playwright to playwright, play to play. They contain a diverse range of moods, atmospheres, histrionics, wit and comedy. For quick reference, the act, scene and page numbers from the Absolute Classics edition are noted; and they are loosely labelled: comedy, dark comedy, light serious and serious as a guide-at-a-glance. The monologues actually mix the introspective, the extrovert, the soliloquy, the descriptive, the compelling, the orated. A monologue is both dependent on its context and yet independent of it. They can be self-contained units existing in their own right. Above all a monologue is to be enjoyed for the immediacy of its language, its situation, its character – its performance. A great monologue captures the essence of character in the moment.

At first sight, some monologues seem more immediate than others. A knowingly ironic speech from a comic maid is clearly appealing. However, a complex tragic soliloquy will be just as rewarding.

We have abridged as little as possible, but if you're using a monologue for an audition, then you might choose to cut and mould a piece to your own individual taste. It's worth bearing in mind the adage that less is more.

Ultimately, a monologue will speak for itself.

II

When Bath's best publisher, Jon Croft, invited us to create the series Absolute Monologues, we were, of course, flattered. As dramaturg and actress we were given *carte blanche* to cut swathes through the great dramatic voices of Western theatre. It was an exciting project, especially given the pleasing number of wonderful women's roles. But it was also pretty daunting.

Yet having been involved in the commissioning of some of these translations as Literary Manager of the Gate Theatre, and having played in some of them, such as Rosaura in Calderón's *Life's a Dream* (La Vida es Sueño), we appreciated their blend of classic text with (often cheeky) contemporary voice. And as theatre-goers, we have all seen the majority of these plays on stage in the past ten years. They are a familiar a part of our generation's repertoire, a generation at ease with its hybrid sense of nationhood and conscious of its pan-European heritage.

It's this broader perspective which partly gives writers the confidence to work with material from countries in whose language they may not be fluent. Though most of the dramatists represented here *do* translate from the original, a few offer versions of a play. Nick Dear, for instance, freely admits he knew no more Russian than 'vodka' when he wrote his version of Ostrovsky's *A Family Affair* (Svoi Lyudi – Sochtsemsya!) for Cheek by Jowl. It's a joyously theatrical version, probably more true to the scurrilous spirit of Ostrovsky than any painstaking 'literal' might be. After all, it's for the theatre that these plays are produced, not for the library.

Neil Bartlett is a performer, director, novelist and translator who speaks fluent French, translating *and* adapting Marivaux and Molière: 'My work has always been concerned with reinventing the past as a way of articulating the present,' he claims. And with characteristic theatricality he proclaims: 'Let us be grand' – 'If translations are to be faithful, they cannot be literal. My translations are very faithful'. The Spanish translator and adaptor David Johnston coined a phrase for this: 'faithful infidelity'. Translations are as much about the modern interpreter's distinctive voice as they are about the original writer's. Ranjit Bolt's Corneille couplets ping out at you; Noel Clark's draw you in. Pip Broughton brings her own sensibility to bear on Zola's *Thérèse Raquin*.

While we must thank all the writers – both living and dead – whose work is represented here, we must also acknowledge all responsibility for any misrepresentation. As far as possible, Jon Croft has helped us avoid any howlers: he's been an encouraging and good-natured guide throughout our journey. Helpful hints also came from Laurence Boswell, Kenneth McLeish, Timothy Walker and Isobel Middleton.

The *frisson* between original writer and his modern interpreter is knowingly summed up in the opening banter between a Duke and his two comic side-kicks in Lope de Vega's *Lost in a Mirror* (El Castigo sin Venganza), adapted by Adrian Mitchell:

Duke:	*Enough nonsense, you fool.*
Febo:	*Sir, he'll feel better for*
	Having a metaphor,
	He's of the fashionable school.
Ricardo:	*You don't like modern poetry?*
	Please accept my apology
	Lock me up in an anthology –
	Throw away the key.
Duke:	*I don't like verse based on pretence.*
	I want reality and playfulness,
	A good story and seriousness –
	But you're all simile and no sense.

In one sense, theatre is only a simile for reality. Yet we can only know what reality is *like* by articulating it through our imaginations. And the the most exciting creative arena for that is theatre.

SIMON READE & ALISON REID
LONDON, 1994

Greek Drama: Euripides

The three Greek tragedians of the 5th Century BC –
Aeschylus, Sophocles and the wilder Euripides – use the
mythological past as a perspective on their own historical
present. The stories and plots upon which their tragedies are
based were well-known to contemporary audiences. The
religious and cultural heritage was laid down in Homeric times
(10th Century BC). What was new was the way the stories
were told and the attitude taken by the playwrights.

Euripides is far more sardonic than his predecessors. His
obsession with the Trojan War in particular shows him using
the desolation of its aftermath as a no-man's-land of human
frailty. Fractured morals and shattered ethics – the human
consequences of war – are laid bare in the ruins of Troy.
Hecuba in *The Women of Troy* chillingly observes:

'The gods planned this: my pain,
My Troy, picked out to hate.
We honoured them for nothing.
Why did they do this, uproot the world?
To make a myth of us,
Give poets a theme for plays?'.

Euripides' uncompromising portraits of his women
protagonists have ironically earned him the reputation for
being a misogynist (the Greek comedy writer Aristophanes
seems to have been the first to make this attack). Yet if we find
Hecuba unforgiving, for example, we should not think her
unforgiveably stubborn in her apparent lack of compassion: her
husband, sons, daughters, have all been ruthlessly assassinated
one-by-one; her City destroyed; and not just her own, but the
dignity of mankind as a whole is lost. Perhaps it is only
through the eyes of such women that Euripides felt able to

share his vision of the world.

Euripides' writing reflects the concerns of his subjects, using single words to express a range of feeling. The translator Kenneth McLeish identifies Euripides' style as allowing the actor 'a great deal of creative space'. McLeish also retains some of the original exclamations, such as 'Fe-oo' or 'O-ee' (often translated melodramatically in the past as 'Alas!', 'Alack!', or 'O Woe is Me!').

McLeish's pared down translations have been partly responsible for revitalising Greek tragedy for a new generation of actors, directors and audiences: Cheek by Jowl's *Philoctetes*; the Manchester Royal Exchange/Claire Benedict *Medea*; the Deborah Warner/Fiona Shaw RSC production of *Electra*; the Gate Theatre's Trojan plays directed by Katie Mitchell and Laurence Boswell with Paola Dionisotti, Barbara Flynn, Kathryn Hunter and Ann Mitchell.

While these are some of the greatest classical roles of Greek antiquity, they are living characters, immediate, who touch the raw nerves of hope and despair.

Women of Troy
(TROADES)

EURIPIDES 414 BC
translated by Kenneth McLeish 1991

Cassandra is King Priam and Queen Hecuba's daughter – the
former dead, the latter awaiting her fate, with all the women of
Troy, as booty of the Trojan war. Queens and princesses will
become slaves. Cassandra, 'Apollo's virgin', has been selected by the
victor Agamemnon as his concubine. To Cassandra's reaction to this
news the Chorus replies:
   'You talk in riddles. You're stripped
   Of everything but misery – and laugh'.
Cassandra has the gift of infallible prophecy and is 'entranced',
possessed, 'gripped by god'.

CASSANDRA
   Rejoice, mother. Crown me with flowers. I've won.
   I'm marrying a king. Take me to him;
   Make me, give me no choice.
   Trust Apollo. If god is god,
   This marriage will ruin His Lordship.
   Agamemnon, grand admiral of Greece!
   I'll hurt him more than Helen did. I'll kill him,
   Strip all his house till the price is paid
   For my father and brothers dead.
   Cassandra, hush! Don't tell it all:
   Don't sing of knives, necks chopped,
   Mine and those others',
   Blood-feud, the mother dead,
   The dynasty destroyed. My marriage-price!
   Sane now, no madness, I tell you this:
   God's words. We outrank the Greeks. We win.
   What did they do? For one woman's sake, one fuck,
   They hunted Helen, squandered a million lives.
   Agamennon – so experienced, so worldly-wise –

Killed what he loved for what he hated,
Threw away happiness, children, home,
For his brother's woman, the wife who left
Of her own free choice, whom no one forced.
So they flocked to the Scamander, lined up to die
On a foreign river's banks, on a foreign plain
For what? Their city? The towers of their native land?
Plucked. They'll never see
Their children; their wives' soft hands
Won't sheet them for burial.
They sleep in foreign soil.
And what of those at home?
Widows, fathers stripped of their sons,
They die alone. Who weeps for them?
Whose offerings drench their tombs?

Now, what of Troy? What of our Trojans, dead
For their native land? What more could they ask?
Spears snatched them. Loving hands, friends' hands,
Carried them home, made them decent for burial.
The earth of Troy enfolds them.
Others escaped, day after day escaped,
To smile on their wives, their children.
What Greek had that?
Is it Hector you weep for, his cruel death?
I tell you, no other man ever died so rich
In reputation – and that was the gift of Greeks.
If they'd stayed at home, who would now know his name?
And Paris. He could have married a nobody,
A name on no one's lips. Instead:
Helen of Sparta, daughter of Zeus on high.
If wars must be fought, a glorious death,
Not a coward's, brings honour to the city.
You see? Mother? Don't weep for Troy.
Don't weep for me. Your enemies, my enemies
I'll marry, and destroy them all.

Women of Troy
(TROADES)

EURIPIDES 414 BC
translated by Kenneth McLeish 1991

Hecuba is the vanquished Queen of Troy, her husband, King
Priam, killed in the war. The victorious Greeks decide how to divide
their booty of Trojan women. Hecuba collapses as Cassandra, her
daughter, is taken away to become Agamemnon's concubine.

HECUBA

No, leave me. I'll lie where I am.
I want no help. Engulfed, overwhelmed –
What else should I do but faint?
O gods! Poor allies,
But who else, what else, is left?
I'll sing my former happiness once more:
How different, how pitiful, what now I bear!
I was queen of Troy; my husband king of kings,
My sons no rank and file but princes, warlords.
What mother in Troy, in Greece,
In all the world, could boast such sons?
One by one I watched the Greeks harvest them.
I chopped my hair for them,
Wept at their tombs. I wept for Priam,
Who sowed them, with these own eyes
Saw him sliced to death at the altar fire.
Saw my city raped. My daughters,
Reared to make royal marriages,
Reared by these hands, I saw them snatched away.
Shall I see them again? Will they see me?
My future's built for me: a wall, a cell.
I'm going to Greece, an old woman, a slave;
I'm to do what I'm told, whatever they decide.
Hector's mother! Shall I keep the door?

Bake bread? Stretch out in the dust,
Ragged body, ragged clothes,
Who once wore silk, who shared the royal bed?

O-ee, what a change is here! For her sake,
That woman's sake, that I be brought to this!
Cassandra, you danced, you spoke with gods –
Now your honour's like water in your hands,
Polyxena, little ones, where are you?
So many little ones, sons, daughters –
Who'll hold me now, who'll comfort me?
Why pick me up? What d'you want of me?
I once walked proud in Troy. No more!
Lead me to slavery. Straw bed, stone pillow.
I'll lie in misery, I'll weep my life away.
Princes! So fortunate!
Call none of us lucky before we die.

Women of Troy
(TROADES)

EURIPIDES 414 BC
translated by Kenneth McLeish 1991

Andromache's husband Hector has died in the Trojan war, a hero
of Troy. Now that the Greeks have won, the women of Troy are
divided up amongst the victors. Andromache's son is to be taken
away by Agamemnon to be slaughtered, 'dashed from the highest
tower': 'no hero's son, he said, should thrive'.

ANDROMACHE
Poor little boy. We loved you so.
We were so proud of you.
Our enemies want to kill you,
To tear your mother's heart.
Your father was a prince. How did that help you?
It brought you this. Why, Hector?
Did I marry you, come here to Troy,
To our marriage-bed – for this?
My son was to rule all Asia,
Not be blood-sacrifice – for Greeks!
Don't cry, darling.
D'you understand what's happening?
You're holding me, clutching me.
Who'll rescue you? Not Hector,
Spear springing from the grave.
Not his brothers, the might of Troy.
You'll fall, break your neck,
Life gone. They'll watch dry-eyed.
Poor baby. Let me hug you tight.
How sweet you smell. Was it for this
I writhed in childbirth, wrapped you,
Gave you my breast to suck – for this?
Hold me, darling. Kiss me. Say goodbye.

Greeks! You count yourselves so civilised –
And this is what you do! An innocent child. Why kill him?
Helen, daughter of Zeus they call you,
But I give you other fathers:
Demons, grudges, blood-lust, death,
Every foulness that sprouts in Earth.
How did Zeus ever father you,
Snail-slime to Greece, to Troy, to all the world?
You glanced our way, those pretty eyes,
Smeared us with death. The plains of Troy!
Take him. Throw him. Drink his blood.

God speaks; my case is heard;
I'm to let my own son die.
Take me to the ship.
I'm to marry a prince,
But first, I'm to lose my child.

Women of Troy
(TROADES)

EURIPIDES 414 BC
translated by Kenneth McLeish 1991

Helen is the curse of Troy. It was her beauty which lured Paris (son
of Queen Hecuba and King Priam of Troy): he stole her from the
Greeks and her husband Menelaus. She is blamed as the cause of the
Trojan war. Now that the Greeks have destroyed Troy, Helen's fate
must be decided. Should Menelaus 'kill her here or ship her home'
to kill her? Helen pleads for her life.

HELEN
You think I'm your enemy. Good arguments or bad,
You won't discuss with me, not face to face.
Never mind. I'll imagine your part, your charges,
And I'll answer them one by one.

She began it, began disaster, giving birth
To Paris – the firebrand, the torch
She dreamt would topple Troy. Her husband,
His ancient majesty, changed the baby's name,
Let 'Alexander' live – disaster for Troy, for me.
Hear what happened next. Three goddesses appeared,
Asked Paris to judge between them. 'Choose me,'
Athene said, 'And your armies will sack great Greece.'
'Choose me,' said Hera, 'And all Asia,
All Europe, will be yours.' Aphrodite next.
She admired my beauty, promised me
To Paris – as soon as she won the prize. She won –
And all that followed, all I and Paris did,
Was to benefit Greece, not Troy.
Is it *you* that strangers rule, spearlords
From overseas? Greece rose; I fell.
I should be wearing a victor's crown.

Instead, I'm sold for my beauty, spat upon.

What do you answer? 'That's not the point.
You betrayed your husband, slipped away.'
When Alexander, Paris, however you name him –
When that criminal, her son, arrived,
A most powerful goddess was at his side –
And you left him behind at home, you fool,
While you sailed to Crete on business!
Well.
Next I question myself, not you.
What was I thinking of? Why did I go
With him, a stranger, leave home,
Betray my friends, my country?
My answer: punish her, punish Aphrodite.
Her power rules even Zeus. How could I resist?
What else? Another charge?
When Paris was killed, when he plunged to Hell,
Our union, ordained by gods, was over:
You'll say I should have left Troy's palace then,
Run to your ships. I tried. They'll tell you,
Gate-keepers, sentries, tower-guards,
Forever catching me as I tried to slip away,
As I lowered myself from the battlements on ropes.

Menelaus, husband, can you kill me?
It's unjust. He made me sleep with him;
Everything I was enslaved me; how could I win?
The gods did this. Do you challenge
Their will, their power? Are you so foolish?

Hecuba
(EKABE)

EURIPIDES 424 BC
translated by Kenneth McLeish 1992

Polyxena is the daughter of Hecuba, the vanquished Queen of
Troy. As the women of Troy wait to be shipped by their captors to
Greece as slaves and concubines, Polyxena's sacrifice is demanded to
honour the dead Greek war-hero Achilles. Odysseus is charged by
the Greek war council to take Polyxena away to her death.

POLYXENA

Do you flinch, my lord? Do you turn away?
Don't worry. I won't beg. I won't embarrass you.
I'll go with you. I'll die. I must.
I want it: only a coward would struggle now.
What use is life to me? My father was king of kings.
That *was* my life. I was a princess,
Brought up for glittering royal marriage.
Kings fought for my hand, to make me queen.
Look at me! Once every woman in Troy,
Old, young, looked up to me. I was a god to them,
Except that gods don't die. Now I'm a slave.
A 'slave'? I can't bear that. I'd rather die.
Who'll buy me, pay money for me – a job lot, perhaps,
'Hector's sister and miscellaneous'? –
Some disciplinarian, wanting his money's worth,
Who'll put me to bread-making, weaving, sweeping floors,
Sharing my bed with some bought-in male
Who'll paddle and paw what princes fought for?
No. Die, rather. Choose to die. Give myself to death.

Take me away, lord. Do what you have to do.
What else have I left? What future? No hope, no joy.
Don't stop me, mother. Don't touch. Don't speak.

Accept my death, a noble death, now,
Before they soil us. We're not used to this.
We could endure the yoke, but not the shame of it,
Not dishonour. No. Better die. Better die.

Hecuba
(EKABE)

EURIPIDES 424 BC
translated by Kenneth McLeish 1992

Hecuba, the vanquished Queen of Troy, has lost her husband King
Priam, her sons, her daughters. Polyxena, her youngest daughter, has
been sacrificed on Achilles' grave by the Greeks. Talthybius, the
Greeks' messenger, has brought report of Polyxena's noble death.

HECUBA
  Polyxena, where am I to look? How am I to weep?
  Pain leapfrogs pain.

  This latest misery, your death, how can I not
  Shed tears? And yet, so royal, so noble –
  To die like that – you take away the sting.
  It's strange. Poor soil, if the gods send rain,
  Bears fertile crops, belies its nature.
  Good soil, deprived of nourishment, grows barren.
  But human nature never changes. Bad is bad,
  Good good, whatever the blows of fate.
  Do we inherit this or learn it? Good we can teach,
  Good upbringing shows that – and if we know good,
  We can use it as a yardstick to measure bad.

  What am I saying? Talthybius, ask the Greeks,
  For me, that no one touch my daughter. Soldiers,
  Sailors, a mass of men, hotter than fire –
  They lead each other on. Indiscipline. Keep them away.

  (to Attendant*)* And you. Take a basin, down to the shore,
  Fill it with water. I'll wash her, the last time,
  Spoiled virgin, bride no-bride. I'll lay her out
  As she deserves. How can I? I've nothing.
  I'll ask my fellow-captives, here in these tents.

They'll give what they can, jewels perhaps,
Snatched up from home, from looters' hands,
They'll give them for Polyxena.
Troy! Palace! Happiness! Priam,
Most blest of princes, blest of fathers,
And I, most blest of mothers. Gone. All gone.
We're old. They've robbed us. Robbed our pride.
Human arrogance! Pride in possessions! Fame!
We preen like cocks on a dunghill. It's nothing.
Ambition, eloquence: nothing. What's happiness?
A life without suffering, day by careful day.

Orestes

EURIPIDES 408 BC
translated by Kenneth McLeish 1993

Electra, and her brother Orestes, have killed their mother
Clytemnestra and her lover. They were appalled that their mother
should not only have cuckolded their father, Agamemnon, while he
was away winning the war against Troy for the Greeks (a war
sparked off by the Trojan kidnap of Menelaus' wife Helen,
Clytemnestra's twin sister), but *then* she killed Agamemnon on his
return.

Six days have gone by since they murdered their mother, and Electra
and Orestes still await their fate: 'Will they kill us by stoning or cut
our throats?'. Hope for a reprieve lies with the anticipated sympathy
of Menelaus, who has just returned from the war. With the black wit
of amorality, hardened by the experience of pain and terror, Electra
explains their predicament.

ELECTRA

Disaster, pain, plague, misery,
Whatever the gods choose to heap on us –
The human condition. We shoulder it.
Tantalus, for example. Zeus' son, they say.
Tantalus the blessed – I'm not making fun of him –
Cowering in midair, stone looming overhead,
Threatening – and why? What for? He was a guest,
They say, a mortal guest at some party of the gods,
And forgot himself. Went too far.
It's dreadful. It happens.

Another one:
Atreus, Tantalus' grandson, Pelops' son –
What else did the spinning Fates choose for him but war?
With his own brother too. Atreus and Thyestes.

I needn't go on. Don't want to go on.
Asks his brother to dinner. Dead baby stew,
Brother's babies.

Passing over what happened next,
We come to Atreus' sons, Agamemnon –
Glorious Agamemnon, if glorious is the word –
And Menelaus. Their mother's name? Aerope:
Aerope the Cretan. Menelaus married Helen
(The one the gods detest), and lord Agamemnon
Married Clytemnestra – a catch, all Greece thought that.
Three girls they had – Chrysothemis, Iphigenia, me
(Electra, yes) – and one boy, Orestes. Agamemnon's
     children,
And hers, that bitch, that foulness,
Who wrapped her own husband in a woven net
And killed him. Why? I'm an innocent virgin,
Know nothing of marriage, it's not for me to say,
You work it out.

So we come to Apollo,
Phoebus Apollo. Not to blame the god,
But he did persuade Orestes to kill his own mother,
Not the most popular crime in all the world.
Orestes did what he was told, what god told him.
I helped, as much as a woman could –
And so did Pylades. He was one of us. He helped.
That's the story so far. That's why Orestes is there,
Poor Orestes, sick on that bed. Raging fever,
Gnawing, hounded into madness by his mother's blood –
I won't speak their names, the goddesses, the Friendly Ones,
Who're hunting him, haunting him ... Six days now,
Six days since we butchered our mother,
Burned her in cleansing fire – and in all that time
He hasn't washed, hasn't eaten. Cowers in those blankets.
When he's not having fits, when he's sane, he sobs.
Then he's up, running, running, an unbridled colt.

They've passed a decree about us, the citizens of Argos:
No one's to shelter us, feed us, speak to us,
The matricides. And today
They're to take a second vote, a community decision:
Will they kill us by stoning, or cut our throats?

Oh, we've hope. We may escape. Menelaus has landed,
Back at last from Troy. His warship's moored by the
        headland.
He got lost, after the war, the Trojan War, got lost,
Wandered everywhere. She's here too, Helen,
Hell to men. He sent her ahead, under cover of darkness,
Didn't want her seen in daylight, by any of those
Whose sons lie dead in Troy, didn't want her stoned.
She's inside, weeping for Clytemnestra (her sister, after all)
And all the other royal disasters. She's all right:
She's got her daughter to comfort her, Hermione,
The child Menelaus left at home when he sailed for Troy —
Brought her here to Sparta, entrusted her
To Clytemnestra, our mother, to bring her up.
Helen has Hermione, she can laugh, forget.
I'm watching the road. This way, that way,
For Menelaus, If he doesn't help us, we're finished.
There's naught so hapless as a Fate-struck house.

The Spanish Golden Age

The three great Renaissance playwrights of the Spanish Golden Age – Lope de Vega, Calderón de la Barca and Tirso de Molina – wrote substantial roles for women. Though these characters sometimes indulge in cross-dressing (like Rosaura in *Life's a Dream*), the expediency of women wearing male attire, as explored by Shakespeare and his contemporaries (who wrote exclusively for male companies) was alien to the 17th century Spanish theatre. In Spain, each company would have as many actresses as actors; and there'd be a leading man (*prima galan*) and a leading lady (*primera dama*) – (both of whom would probably be prima donnas). Apart from the posh theatre-goers, who could co-mingle in boxes, men and women were otherwise segregated – so an actress might address her section of the crowd when appropriate.

The plays generally explore: Religion (the Catholic themes of fate and free will – Tirso de Molina was a monk; Calderón and Lope took minor orders after long, dilettante lives); Love; and, being Mediterranean, Honour. Men choose to be restricted by it (but are slippery with its codes). Women are just restricted by it. Honour is hybrid, synonymous with rank, esteem, pride, status and, most importantly, a woman's chastity – all of which become concerns of Honour when they become part of the public domain. These playwrights expose the hypocrisy of a man who loses his 'honour' when his daughter or sister is raped by a man of honour (an aristocrat or a high ranking official). One King, in Tirso de Molina's *The Last Days of Don Juan,* complains: 'How little we must value our honour, that we leave it in women's care'. And the playwrights highlight the injustice suffered by the dishonoured woman: 'My reputation lies in tatters, among my petticoats,' says one of Don Juan's victims. To appease the male sense of honour, a violated woman is either obliged to marry the very man who dishonoured her, or is conveniently locked away in a convent (out of sight, out of mind). Though women have a place in society, men outrageously insist that they should know it.

Aside from the comic roles, Love and (dis)Honour are the themes in the monologues which follow. The voices of the Spanish Golden Age translators and adaptors of the late 20th century are as strong as the playwrights' of the early 17th century. So, Nick Dear and David Johnston have much fun with the bright naivety of Tisbea and Ines – one claiming quite erotically to have been 'untouched by love'; the other head-over-heels in it. Love, of course, is also a sickness – hence Aurora's jealousy; and causes extreme problems – the young Casandra having married a gadabout unfaithful Duke, only to have fallen in love with his bastard son, her stepson. Love involves sex but sex is debased by men's untrammeled lust – both Isabel and Laurencia are raped. The former is partly concerned with her father's loss of honour (there's blind loyalty for you), whereas the latter confronts an impotent male community in anguish.

The Last Days of Don Juan
(EL BURLADOR DE SEVILLA Y CONVIDADO DE PIEDRA)

TIRSO DE MOLINA 1616-1625
adapted by Nick Dear 1990

Tisbea is a knowing innocent who lives in a small fishing village on
the Spanish coast of Tarragona. Later, her friend sings:

'A lass went to the ocean for
To fish with nets and poles;
She caught no fish, but hauled ashore
A thousand lovers' souls'.

Spain. A seashore. Enter Tisbea, *with a fishing pole.*

TISBEA
Of all the girls who live along this shore,
Of all the girls who play in the curling waves,
Of all the girls of Tarragona, whose rose
And jasmine feet dance in the hot, white sand –
I am the only one
Untouched by love.

Here, where the sun wakes
And creeps across the sea, lighting
Sapphire-blue peaks on the water;
Here where every grain of sand's a pearl,
A particle of sunshine;
Here is where I live.
I hear the romance of the sea-birds, the cries
Of dippers and waders,
The sighs of the waves on the rocks,
And I feel not a lick
Of desire.

My fishing pole is my greatest joy.

This supple rod, that whips and bends
With the wriggles of hooked fishes.
Some days I take my net and snare the crabs
And shellfish of the shady pools, dark places
Thick with mystery. For I'm at peace.
The serpent tongue of love's unknown to me.
My heart is free.

When my girlfriends and I set sail in a skiff
Upon the raging ocean,
They tell me of their aching hearts, hot dreams,
Infatuations.
Well, I have to laugh.
Poor victims of love.

Love hunts for me but I slip his nets.
I sleep on in my simple hut;
The danger passes over.
I like my hut, it's a
Cathedral of thatch, with a spire of smoke,
A choir of bright cicadas. In there
My virtue is preserved in straw,
Like ripe fruit, or
Delicate crystal.

The brave Tarragonian fishermen, who defend
Our coast from pirates,
All fancy me to death.
But I reject them, every one.
They make such crude suggestions.
I find it a help to go suddenly deaf
And turn to stone, for then
They quit their advances
And leave me alone.

Anfriso is the nicest.
The muscles on him – goodness!
He speaks well, he can read and write, he's brave,

He gives to beggars. If things go bad for Anfriso,
He just carries on filleting flatfish, shrugs,
And grins his grin.
A truly lovely man! But –
Hangs round my cottage in all weathers.
Leaves poems pinned on trees.
Starves himself.
I see him out there shivering, in icy wind
And rain, playing his pan-pipes right
Through the night, just for me!
Only for me!

I ignore him, of course.
I am a tyrant, aren't I?

The other girls can sigh for him, and die for him,
And drown themselves in perfume, but I,
His chosen, give him naught but pain.
This is love's triumph.
To never know when you are beaten.
To clutch at empty air.
To adore where despised
And despise where adored.
To wound, humiliate and – oh ! What a waste
Of breath, to talk of love
When you could be fishing –
Please, just leave me to bait my hook
With a squirming worm or a lump of squid,
And cast far out to –
Look! What's that?

A sinking ship!
Sails like a peacock's tail, fanned out
With pomp and pride!
But it's struck a reef, bound for the bottom!
Two people have leaped overboard!
Down goes the hulk with a roar!
Now only the tip of the mainmast's left –

The wind in the topsail thrashing
Like a wild thing locked in a cage!
Now one of them's carrying the other one, swimming
So bravely through the surf – they've gone down!
No, they surface!
They're gaining the shore!
They're sucked under!
Please God, don't let those people die!
(calls) Anfriso! A shipwreck!
Coridon, Alfredo!
Come quick, help the survivors!

(ACT I, SCENE III; PP 15-18)

The Last Days of Don Juan
(EL BURLADOR DE SEVILLA Y CONVIDADO DE PIEDRA)

TIRSO DE MOLINA 1616–1625
adapted by Nick Dear 1990

Don Juan, yet again, has been caught *in flagrante* with a young
noblewoman in Naples. To avoid the repercussions, he flees with
assorted equeries and grooms by ship – which, thanks to a 'dreadful
whirlwind', sinks just off the Spanish coast of Tarragona. All are
drowned, save Don Juan – and a Cook, **Catalina**.

Enter from the sea Catalina *carrying* Don Juan.

CATALINA
Someone, give us a drink of wine! The sea's far too damn
salty. I don't mind a little salt with my eggs, but this is
absurd! Not only could you drown out there, you could
end up pickled as well! All right if you like sardines, I
suppose, but I don't. You'd've thought God would've had
the sense to mix a little white wine with his ocean – make it
a bit more palatable for the drowning. I can't stand water at
the best of times – but salted water! Ugh! ... Master? Oh
Lord, he's as cold as ice! Master! Wake up! – Like a wet rag.
Is he dead? The sea done this, but knowing my luck, I'll
swing for it. Bleeding stupid idea, putting bits of old wood
on the water, and expecting them to float. As for that damn
needle they spend so much time staring at, with the little N
at one end and the little S at the other, well, if that's what
they use for their canvas, no wonder the sails blew away!
And now look at us! Shipwrecked!

(ACT I, SCENE III; P 18)

The Last Days of Don Juan
(El Burlador de Sevilla y Convidado de Piedra)

Tirso de Molina 1616-1625
adapted by Nick Dear 1990

Fishing on the Tarragonian coast, where she lives simply and
innocently, **Tisbea** has seen a sinking ship. The only survivors, a
cook and Don Juan, have been welcomed by the village. Tisbea has
fallen in love with him, despite her suspicion that 'all men are traitors
and liars'. Because Don Juan promises to marry her, she lets him lie
with her in her hut.

Enter Tisbea *dishevelled.*

TISBEA
Fire! Fire! My hut's in flames! My tears won't put them out!
My humble home is burning like a town destroyed by war!
I thought my walls were hard. I thought I was made of
rock. But the fury of love burns even stone, engulfs my
house of straw!

Fetch water! I'm ablaze! Have mercy, love, you scorch my
soul!

My cottage is a place of wickedness. I was deflowered there
– left hot and red and bleeding in that oven of desire. My
guest was false! Oh monstrous boy! He's stolen my honour,
and fled! May the sparks of dying stars fall on his head, and
burn his hair with shame!

Yes, it happened to me! The one that mocked all men. He
came like a cloud in off the sea, and darkened my nights and
days. Don Juan! – he tricked his way into my bed. I was so
proud! Now I'm nothing. Disgrace rains down on me.

He even took the horses! I want my revenge! ... I'll follow him. I'll walk to Seville. I'll throw myself before the King, and beg for justice!

Fire! Fire! My soul's on fire! The world's on fire! Fire!

(ACT I, SCENE V; P 28)

Fuente Ovejuna

LOPE DE VEGA 1612-1614
adapted by Adrian Mitchell 1988

The peasants of a small, rural town are oppressed by a tyrannical
Commander. He takes advantage of his position, forcing the local
women into his bed. One woman resists him – **Laurencia**, with the
help of her fiancé Frondoso – which enrages the Commander. When
Laurencia marries, the Commander violently bursts in on the
wedding and arrests both Laurencia and her husband. While the
village elders are worrying over what to do, Laurencia returns.

Enter Laurencia, *dishevelled*.

LAURENCIA
Out of my way and let me in
To this all-wise, all-male Council meeting.
You may not allow a woman to vote
But you can't stop her yelling.

Don't you know me, for God's sake?
Hard to recognise me, isn't it,
The state I'm in?
You let those soldiers take me
Without lifting a finger.
You left it to Frondoso
To protect me when that's a father's job
Till after the wedding night.
For, even if you buy a diamond ring
It isn't yours till it's on your finger.
So why did Frondoso have to run
The gauntlet of those vicious troops?
When the Commander took me off
You stood and goggled like cowardly shepherds
While the wolf ran off with your lamb.

Oh, did they hold you back with swords?
Well, they held me down with violent abuse,
With violent threats, with violent hands,
With every kind of violence
So he could violate me.

Doesn't my hair tell its own story?
Can you see the blood on my skirt?
Can you see the bruises
Where they clutched me?
Where they hit me?
Can you see anything at all?

Call yourselves respected councillors?
Call yourselves my kinsmen?
Your guts should burst out of your bellies
To see Laurencia like this.

Fuente Ovejuna – the spring for sheep.
Sheep, that's all you are, a flock of sheep.
Sheepspring's the right name for this town.
Give me your weapons
You're a heap of stones,
A shelf of plaster idols,
A knot of cold-hearted snakes –
No, that's not fair on snakes –
A snake at least
Follows the hunters who steal its eggs
And lashes out, biting into their legs,
Injecting venom before they can reach
The safety of their saddles.

You gang of rabbits – stay down your holes!
Ancient cockerels, loafing around the dunghill
While other men screw your wives.
Give me your swords.
Take my sewing needles.

My God, do we women have to show you
How to smash those bastards
And wash yourself clean in a trough of their blood?

Stones! Rabbits! Sheep! Eunuchs!

Tomorrow we women will dress you up
In our best skirts and blouses.
We'll paint and powder you prettily
And lead you round the houses.

Listen, the Commander has made up his mind
To murder Frondoso at his headquarters.
There'll be no trial. There'll be no verdict.
And maybe his body will be found in the river.
And maybe his body will never be found.

And when the Commander takes the rest of you,
One by one, week by week, and strings you up
While your fellow-councillors hold secret meetings –
I'll be laughing my head off – little boys!
O when he's killed all the men of this town
Then the age of Amazons will return
And women will show the world what courage means.

(ACT III, SCENE I; PP 76-78)

The Gentleman from Olmedo
(EL CABALLERO DE OLMEDO)

LOPE DE VEGA 1620-1625
translated & adapted by David Johnston 1991

Ines has been laboriously courted for two years by Don Rodrigo, in her father's garden:
> *'all his efforts, sighs and pleading*
> *leave me unmoved, as cold as ice'.*

Don Alonso, a noble *caballero*, has been visiting Medina's Fair, where he's seen the fair Ines. She's seen him too and thinks he's gorgeous. Their subsequent secret wooing all takes place under cover of night because Don Rodrigo's already asked Dona Ines' father for her hand in marriage.

INES

Alonso, you've been gone so long
that time itself seemed to stand still.
Rodrigo has been here again.
My heart belongs to you alone.
There is no force on this wide earth
that could ever keep us apart,
or stop me from being your wife.

I went walking in the garden
last night, alone,
I poured out my heart to the trees,
to the fountains and the flowers,
feeling so lonely that I wept.
For nature lives in harmony
with nature, and bright day follows
dark night for life and love to grow.
But I live in eternal night
waiting for the sun of my life
to dawn. I must be going mad

– I fancied a lily replied:
'Ines, why torment yourself so?
The sun that you worship appears
to you at night, do not complain.
His beauty is all the brighter;'

And so I come to this dark place,
like a moth hungry for your light;
the flame in which I live and die,
in which I am consumed and burn
and in which I am born again.

(ACT II; PP 115-116)

Lost in a Mirror
(EL CASTIGO SIN VENGANZA)

LOPE DE VEGA 1631
adapted by Adrian Mitchell

Young **Casandra** has married the older Duke of Ferrara. She is
unhappy with him and soon falls in love with his bastard son, Count
Federico. Federico has also fallen for Casandra and is now miserable
and sullen as he knows it is an impossible match. Neither is fully aware
of the other's love. Casandra misinterprets his behaviour, believing that
he is unhappy because he will lose his claim to the Duke's wealth and
titles if she has any children. She attempts to ease his worries.

CASANDRA
I believe my marriage
To the Duke's the cause of this deep dejection
And misery of yours.
Because, if I should bear his son
All your hopes will be undone –
Federico – a lost cause.

Now since it's I who cause you this
Spiritual agony,
Let me disillusion you –
You will never see
Any brother usurp your throne.
The Duke's a husband for one reason alone –
That's what his subjects want him to be.

The Duke's debaucheries –
I'm trying to be polite,
Have allowed him to be in my arms
For less than one short night,
Although, according to his jeers,
It felt more like a hundred years.

After this very brief respite
He has returned to his old haunts
With renewed lust, of course.
He broke the bridle of my arms
Like a spirited, wild horse
Who shies suddenly and rears
When the drumbeat hurts his ears.
(I try, you see, not to be coarse).
And the horse bolts, scattering round
Trappings of fine embroidery,
Pieces of bridle and the bit,
Spraying like foam and flashing by,
There go the reins, there goes the bridle,
There go the straps, there goes the saddle –
There goes the Duke, having broken free
From the bonds of matrimony,
Let loose on the women of the town,
Scattering fragments of his fame.
Here he leaves his title behind,
There, he scatters his good name,
The honour of his ancestry,
His body's health, his bravery –
Gambled away in this deadly game.
He wastes his time, he wastes himself,
He turns night into day
With his despicable ribaldry.

So please believe me when I say
You will inherit his estate
For Federico, I shall write
To my fierce father, begging him
To come and set me free
From this palace prison
Unless death comes first to me
And ends all my misery.

(ACT II; PP 134-135)

Lost in a Mirror
(EL CASTIGO SIN VENGANZA)

LOPE DE VEGA 1631
adapted by Adrian Mitchell

Young **Casandra** marries the older Duke of Ferrara. He is faithful to
her for one night only, spending all other nights debauching himself
with the women in the town. Casandra falls in love with the Duke's
bastard son, Count Federico, and he with her. She knows this is
dishonourable but she can not quell her feelings towards her stepson.

CASANDRA
Step softly, love, picking your way between
Injuries, revenge and indecisions
And these dishonourable hopes of mine.
On impossible foundations
You can't build a house of happiness.
Because of the wrongs done by the Duke
My soul leans towards wickedness,
I'm like a madwoman, trying to take
Revenge and pleasure at the same time
By committing the greatest possible crime.
The noble, prudent Count will be
The key to open revenge's gates
But there must be total secrecy
Because the felony's so great.
I can read Federico's mind,
It trembles in the balance.
It is most easy to understand
A man who speaks through silence.
My soul loves his uneasiness.
Since the Duke gives me reason
There is a voice inside me says:
Such love can be no treason.

And should I surrender hopelessly
To such a fine man, I believe
The last woman to fall would not be me
Nor the last one to deceive.
History tells us of many daughters
Who fell in love with fathers.
My position's not inhuman –
Sisters have loved their brothers.
Yet precedents for evil
Cannot grant me permission.
To quote an old example
Can't justify my passion.

Enough of this –
The Count is here.
My mind's made up.
Why should I fear?

(ACT II; PP 147-148)

Lost in a Mirror
(EL CASTIGO SIN VENGANZA)

LOPE DE VEGA 1631
adapted by Adrian Mitchell

Aurora is betrothed to Count Federico, the Duke of Ferrara's
bastard son. Since the arrival of the Duke's new young wife,
Casandra, Federico has been melancholy because he has fallen in love
with his father's bride. To try and snap him out of this by inspiring
his jealousy, Aurora flirts with Carlos, the Marques de Gonzaga, but
this backfires when Frederico says that if she loves the Marquis, then
she can have him.

The Duke departs to fight a Holy War – Frederico and Casandra are
unable to control their passion for each other. Aurora sees all and
everything become crystal clear to her.

The Duke*'s palace. Enter* Aurora *and* Carlos.

AURORA

I loved the Count and he loved me,
But he was wilier than Ulysses.
With time our love grew strong. It bloomed.
Then he rode off to fetch Cassandra.
I expected that we'd be married
When he returned from Mantua.
I trusted all his promises –
How womanly to trust a man!
But when Frederico did come home,
He was all melancholy and wan,
The Duke suggested he should be
Married to me, as I proposed.
But Frederico claimed that he
Had, in my fondness, been replaced
By you. He tried to escape from me

As lovers do, when loving ends,
And claiming that you gave him grounds.
Jealousy made as much a mark on him
As jealousy makes on a diamond.
Where love does not exist at all
Jealousy cannot touch the mind.
When Frederico rejected me
I became as stern as steel.
Now jealousy's a sharp-eyed lynx
Can see through a stone wall.
That's how I made my discovery.
There are two arched recesses
In Casandra's dressing room
Covered with looking glasses
Instead of tapestries.
Helped by the many mirrors there
A watching eye may roam
Through a complete reflection of
What seems a second room,
Identical but then reflected back
Into another mirror, so there seem
A hundred bright receding rooms
And every one the same.
Suspicion cannot be controlled.
Two rooms from them I stood, all ice,
And looked and saw a dreadful sight
In the crystal looking-glass –
His lips, upon her rosy lips,
Delicately alighting.
My soul drained out of me, I ran
Sobbing aloud my mind's misfortune
And the misfortune of two who love
Blindly, while the Duke's away,
So they compete in love and scorn,
Delighting in greater audacity
Than you could find in infidels
Or cannibals, people-eating horrors
Who sea-dogs love to yarn about.

It seemed to me that the mirrors,
Which showed the pair one hundred times,
Darkened their brilliant embrace
As if to hide such a shameless crime.
Then from their lips, their love moved on
To manifold, hundredfold caresses,
And watched every single one,
Those ventures of sinful kisses.

They say the Duke is riding home,
Laurel-crowned, like a second Mars.
He fought on behalf of the Shepherd of Rome
And scattered all his enemies.
Tell me, Carlos, what can I do?
I'm terrified that you will leave me.
Your words of love, were they really true,
Or, like the Count, will you deceive me?

(ACT III; PP 152-153)

The Mayor of Zalamea
(EL ALCADE DE ZALAMEA)

CALDERON 1642
adapted by Adrian Mitchell 1981

Billeted in Zalamea, the Captain has become besotted with a rich
farmer's daughter, **Isabel**:

'I thought I'd find some bumpkin wench –
I discovered a fine lady'.

He kidnaps her and rapes her in the forest.

The forest. Isabel *is alone, weeping.*

ISABEL

I never want to see the light
The lovely light, ever again,
I never want to see myself,
My shameful self, ever again.
Night sky, with your dark blue meadows
Bright with a million star-flowers,
Don't let the dawn walk towards me
With that young sunshine smile of hers.
If you can't keep the dawn away,
Let her come with eyes full of rain,
Not mocking me with laughing light.

King of all planets, mighty Sun,
Just for this once, wait down below
The cold sea a little longer.
Just for this once, let the shy night
Rule her shining, trembling empire
A little longer, hiding me.
Sun-God, let it be said of you:
He listened to her graciously
And, because he decided to

He granted everything she asked.
Why do you want to rise at all
To read my story – this cruel,
Cold-blooded act, a tale as vile
As has been told about the way
Men revenge themselves on women?

No? You're a tyrant. Even as I
Beg you to delay arriving
A little longer, here you come,
 Striding along, face towering
Over the trees' tall green shadows.
I've angered you. You've been plotting.
You're part of the conspiracy
To cut my honour into shreds.
What can I do? Where can I go?
If home, my father's wide
Wound will gape wider, horribly.
How he loved to see his honour.
Reflected in the moon of mine.
Moon ... a bad sun has eclipsed her,
My honour's blotted out. No light.
And if I don't go home, from fear
And from respect for him – they'll say
I encouraged my attacker
And call me hypocritical.

My brother came by here just now.
I ran away. I should've stayed.
I should have stayed and let him know
What happened to me. And I should
Have let him, in his righteous rage,
Kill me. I'll shout to him. He'll come
And kill me, kill me right away.
I'll scream out what's been done to me
Until it echoes –

(ACT III; PP 65-66)

Life's a Dream
(LA VIDA ES SUEÑO)

CALDERON 1635
adapted by Adrian Mitchell & John Barton 1983

Rosaura has arrived in Poland from Muscovy, dressed as a man.
She's pursuing Astolfo, Duke of Muscovy, who stole her honour
when he swore to marry her but then absconded to Poland for the
rich and powerful Princess Estrella.

Rosaura has never met her father, but knows he is a nobleman in
Poland. She decides to trust Clotaldo, who has saved her life, and
tells him her story. (Unknown to her, she has found her father. He is
Clotaldo.)

ROSAURA

I am not what I seem,
This is show, disguise, a costume.
My name is Rosaura.

I had a noble mother
In the court of Muscovy.
A deceiver wooed and won her.
I do not know his name
For she would never tell me,
But I think he was valiant
Because I sometimes feel
His courage in myself.
He told her the old story:
He'd be true to her,
He would marry her.
But one day he left her:
She was too low-born
For his nobility.
From this loose knot

I came into the world,
And so in time her tale
Was told again in me.

Astolfo is the man
Who despoiled my honour.
He swore he'd marry me
And for a little while
I thought I was happy.
Suddenly he left.
He came here to Poland
To marry his Estrella.
As a star first joined us
So a star destroyed us.

I wept within.
I was mocked,
I was angry,
I was mad,
I was dead,
I was ... me ...
Babel ... Muddle ... Hell.

Pain is felt, not words
But my mother understood.
When you know the person
To whom you tell your weakness
Has been weak herself,
It's as if you are both lost
In the same strange country.
That is a comfort.
She said, "Go to Poland,
Either make him marry you
Or kill him. Kill him with
Your father's sword."
I swore that.
She dressed me as a man

And said, "Show this sword
To the noble men in Poland,
One of them will know it
And be kind to you
Because you are his child."

I want to meet my father
And tell him how I hate him.
It is because of him
That my Astolfo left me.
He said he could not marry
A girl who had no father
And did not know his name.
Hate is a clear thing.
Though I am in the darkness
I am clear about my father.

(ACT I, SCENE II; PP 107-109)

Life's a Dream
(LA VIDA ES SUENO)

CALDERON 1635
adapted by Adrian Mitchell & John Barton 1983

Rosaura is secretly in Poland to stop Duke Astolfo marrying
Princess Estrella – he fled from Rosaura, dishonouring her. She had
vowed to marry or kill Astolfo, but is now determined to kill him.
Sigismund is at war with his father, the King of Poland, for denying
his existence since birth and thus denying his rightful inheritance of
the throne. Rosaura and Sigismund have met twice before: once
when she arrived in Poland in the mountains, dressed as a man,
where Sigismund was incarcerated by his father; and then in the
King's palace, when Rosaura was dressed as a woman, and Sigismund
had been allowed to taste kingship for a day, but had proved to be as
wild as the stars had predicted at his birth, attacking Rosaura. Now
they meet for a third time.

ROSAURA

Honour: I wish to speak to you of honour.
Be generous, Sigismund. Your fame has sprung
From night's dim shadows into royal day,
And as the sun leaps from the arms of dawn
And bathes the hills and paints the shining sea-foam,
So may you now, that are the sun of Poland,
Shine upon me, a poor unhappy woman.

Three times we've met.
Three times you haven't known me.
First, I was a man
When you lay in prison
And your story eased me.
Second, I was a woman
When you were a King,
A dream King, a shadow.

Now I am whole,
I am both man and woman.
I had a love in Muscovy.
He is the Duke Astolfo.
He swore to marry me
But he broke his oath:
I seek revenge on him
As you seek it today
Against your royal father.

I wear both silk and steel.
Both of us wish to destroy this marriage.
I, that the man who is my lawful husband
May not be married to another woman;
You, to prevent Poland and Muscovy
Joining in one. Then as I am a woman,
Help me to win my honour. As I am man,
I say, go and seize on Poland's crown;
Destroy Astolfo, do not let him have it.
Yet as I am woman, I beseech your pity
And pray you will be gentle now and kind.
Yet as I'm man, I offer you my sword.
But if you touch me as I am a woman,
Then as I am a living breathing man,
I will defend my honour like a man
And I will kill you. In this war of love
I am a woman in my woe and fury,
But as I am a man, I'm strong for honour.

(ACT III, SCENE III; PP 151-152)

Seventeenth Century France

17th century French drama established classical codes of comedy and tragedy which subsequently permeated the whole of European theatre. Though the names of Molière (comedy) and Racine (tragedy) are the most well-known to us, it was Corneille (comedy *and* tragedy) who established the parameters of both classical genres. His boisterous comedies sparkle with wit; his sincere tragedies elegantly, yet passionately examine the conflicts between private love and public duty.

Dryden, in England's Restoration, was the first of many commentators to shy away from French tragedy as untranslatable because of its rhyming couplets – English tragedians have always been more fond of blank verse. Where zestful rhyme appeals in comedy, it might not always be assumed to be appropriate for tragedy by English-speaking performers. Thus Noel Clark's tragic couplets in his Corneille translations and Neil Bartlett's in Racine's *Bérénice,* are as considerable an achievement and challenge to the perfomer as Bartlett's and Ranjit Bolt's dazzling rhymes in Molière's comedies.

Bartlett writes his Molière and Racine translations phonetically so that you can see how they scan (so 'prare' is one syllable where 'prayer' would be two). Of this twelve syllable form he says: 'I want the audience to be aware at all times that these texts are a mapping of modern language and modern theatre over the language and theatre of another time and place. I want them to sound both English and foreign'.

Polyeuct

PIERRE CORNEILLE 1642
translated by Noel Clark 1991

Pauline dreamt that her husband, Polyeuct, would die at the hands
of her former lover Severus and her father Felix, Rome's Govenor in
Armenia.

Polyeuct, encouraged by his friend Nearchus, is secretly baptised a
Christian, and then publicly mocks the priests and their gods in the
pagan Roman temple. Felix is outraged and sentences his son-in-law
to death, telling Pauline that 'gods and Emperor outrank family'.
Pauline pleads with Polyeuct to repent, and with her father to
forgive him – neither shows remorse. Polyeuct is executed –
martyred – and in that moment Pauline is converted to Christianity.

PAULINE

Barbaric father, finish off your work;
A second worthy victim waits. Don't shirk:
Your daughter with your son-in-law dispatch!
For you, in crime or virtue, we're a match
And your barbarity is justified!
My husband's faith he left me as he died:
His blood your executioners shed on me
Opened my eyes, enabled me to see.
I know! I believe! God's truth I've realised:
Look! In my husband's blood, I've been baptised!
Christian at last! No point in disputation!
Execute me! Save your rank and station!
Beware of the Emperor – and Severus, too:
Unless you want to die, my death is due.
Polyeuct calls me to that happy end;
I see Nearchus welcome arms extend.
Take me before your gods whom I detest –
They toppled only one, I'll smash the rest!

You'll see me challenge all you hold most frightening –
Jupiter's puny, painted bolts of lightning!
In saintly revolt against parental tie,
For once, my filial duty I'll defy.
Nor is it grief that urges me to dare:
God's grace it is that moves me – not despair!
I am a Christian, father – need I repeat?
By putting me to death, our bliss complete!
For both of us, that stroke will prove its worth:
Securing *me* in heaven, *you* on earth!

(ACT V; P 206)

Cinna

PIERRE CORNEILLE 1640
translated by Noel Clark 1992

Emilia's father was murdered by Augustus on his way to becoming
Emperor of Rome. Emilia is intent on revenge and has made Cinna
– her lover and Augustus' confidant – swear to assassinate Augustus.
Only then will she marry him.

EMILIA
A father's death must be repaid in kind:
The thirst for righteous vengeance sears my mind!
You wilful offspring of outraged devotion –
Blindly embraced in my distraught emotion,
You fierce demands that swamp my self-control –
Grant a few moments' respite to my soul!
Let me consider in this situation,
What is at stake and what my destination.
Seeing Augustus, clothed in all his glory,
I cannot but recall the tragic story
Of how my father's death, at Caesar's hand,
Was his first step to tyrannise this land!
When memory revives that gory scene –
Source of my hatred, outcome of his spleen –
Then heart and soul I yield to vengeful lust,
Thinking a thousand dead for one were just!
Yet, in my feverish pursuit of justice,
Cinna I love, more than I hate Augustus!
I feel my surging rage turn to cold dread,
Knowing revenge may cost my lover's head.
I'm angry with myself for Cinna's sake –
Chilled by the risks I'm forcing him to take.
Though Cinna's fearless, serving me alone,
To bid him shed that blood's to risk his own!
Who could effect an Emperor's execution

Without attracting storms of retribution?
The danger's certain, far less sure the end:
Betrayal only needs one treacherous friend.
A plan ill-laid, mistimed – and all's revealed!
The plot misfires and Cinna's fate is sealed
He's ruined ... even with the tyrant dead!
Though Cinna, for my sake, would hazard all,
The Emperor could crush him in his fall.
Cinna, your death would be too high a price –
You'd not avenge me by self-sacrifice!
Cruel is the heart to which benign appears
A love foredoomed to drown in bitter tears!
Should one not reckon as the direst woe,
An enemy's death which caused such tears to flow?
But why should filial vengeance make me weep?
In such a cause, what price would not seem cheap?
Even should the assassin's life be lost,
What right has one to haggle at the cost?

Vain fears! Affection's craven voice, be still!
Cease your ignoble onslaught on my will!
Love, whose unwelcome care's to blame, must bow
To duty's call, not undermine my vow!
To yield is triumph; to prevail, disgrace:
Let duty rule! Love – graciously give place!
Love, claiming less, duty shall more accord –
And duty's triumph then be love's reward!

(ACT I; PP 83-84)

Cinna

PIERRE CORNEILLE 1640
translated by Noel Clark 1992

Emilia has made her lover Cinna swear that he will kill the Roman
Emperor Augustus, in revenge for Augustus' murder of her own
father Once Cinna does this, she will marry him. Augustus hears of a
plot against him and calls upon Cinna for advice, for which he
rewards Cinna by giving him Emilia. Cinna now questions whether
he can kill Augustus. Lady Macbeth-like, Emilia chastises Cinna:
'Caesar has unmanned you'.

EMILIA

You play the tyrants' game if you just wait
For bolts of lightning to decide their fate!
Go, serve your tyranny! What's left to say?
Allow your craven soul to have its way!
And to restore your wavering spirit's calm,
Forget your birth, forget Emilia's charm!
My fury I'll assuage without your hand:
I shall avenge my father and our land!
I might have died a noble death, in fact,
But love forbade me carry out the act.
For love it was that held me as your slave,
Compelling me, for you, my life to save.
Had I dispatched the tyrant on my own,
I'd have been slain by soldiers round the throne.
Depriving you of heart already yours.
Since love for your sake bade me live, take pause...
I did so, vainly hoping you might prove –
By noble action, worthy of my love...
The gods forgive me! Clearly, I was wrong
It's to Pompey's grandson I belong!
By false appearances I was misled:
My heart I squandered on a slave instead!

But I still love you, be you what you may...
If gaining me, your master you'd betray,
A thousand others, all too readily,
Would pay the price you spurned, to marry *me*!
But none shall take your place, however brave!
Live for your tyrant; I shall die your slave!
My days, like, are numbered; few they'll be!
Since cowardice forbids you merit me,
Come, watch me die, bathed in his blood and mine –
Virtue, my sole companion in decline –
You'll hear my dying whisper, mind at rest:
"Do not blame fate; it's you who failed the test!
I now await my tomb – condemned by you:
The glory mine, which should have been your due!
Power absolute I've crushed, the tyrant killed...
But I'd be yours alive, if you'd so willed..."

(ACT III; PP 115-116)

Le Cid

PIERRE CORNEILLE 1637
translated by Noel Clark 1993

Chimena is in love with Rodrigo. But Rodrigo has murdered
Chimena's father to avenge his own father's honour after the two old
men had quarrelled. Chimena still loves Rodrigo but goes to the
King to beg for justice because she believes that her father's death
can not go unavenged.

CHIMENA

My father's dead; I watched the life-blood flow
From the most distinguished warrior I know –
Blood, to save your walls, so often shed –
Blood, which your crown to countless victories led –
Blood, still steaming with indignant fire
At not being spilled to feed your glory, Sire!
With blood, that all war's perils dared not claim,
Rodrigo's soaked your soil – in honour's name!
I hurried there, pale, faint with disbelief,
And found him lifeless. Sire, forgive my grief!
Words fail me to pursue this awesome tale;
My tears and sighs may be of more avail...

... My woe is more than honoured by your vow.
I found him dead, Sire, as I said just now –
His side a gaping wound. To win my trust,
His blood had writ my duty in the dust;
Or rather, his great valour, thus laid low,
Besought me, by that wound, to let you know,
Most just of monarchs! Borrowing my voice,
Those pleading lips have left me with no choice:
Sire, suffer not, so long as you shall reign,
That here at home such license should obtain
As to expose great men without redress

To blows inflicted by foolhardiness
While youthful hotheads vilify their name,
Bathe in their blood, their memory defame.
So brave a warrior as the one you've lost –
Unless avenged – much loyalty will cost.
Father's been killed and vengeance I request,
Less for myself, than in your interest!
You've suffered by the death of one so great!
So, let his equal share my father's fate –
And sacrifice him, not to me, but you –
To crown, to grandeur and your person, too –
For good of all the State, I beg you, Sire:
Condemn the one who boasts a deed so dire!

(ACT II, SCENE IV; PP 36-37)

SERIOUS 65

sion

(N COMIQUE)

PIERRE CORNEILLE 1635
translated & adapted by Ranjit Bolt 1989

Lyse is maid to the rich and powerful Isabelle. Lyse and Clindor, a manservant, are in love; but Clindor wants to be rich, and thus encourages the affections of Isabelle towards him. Lyse is incensed by Clindor's fickle promises.

LYSE

You bastard! To pretend to love someone
Because they're pretty, and it might be fun!
I suppose what I feel's irrelevant,
As long as you can play at being "gallant".
Opening your heart – to show me that it's false;
So hot for me you're marrying someone else!
Well, chop your heart in two (I wish you would) –
It isn't going to do you any good:
You wait until my mistress gets to hear
She's just a stepping stone in your career!
I "banter" with you, but it's all to hide
The hate and anger boiling up inside:
Revenge is hardly something you announce –
Panthers'll wait for hours before they pounce –
Setting a trap needs stealth, and careful thought –
I'm going to have a field-day when you're caught!

(a mischievous chuckle mounts to evil laughter before subsiding, comically, into blubbering. She pulls out a handkerchief, blows her nose and addresses the audience)

But what's he done that I'm so furious at?
Feathered his nest? There's nothing wrong with that.
He does love me – he just loves money more –

These days, that's not worth hating someone for!
And then, all that about necessity:
There's something in it – should I leave him be?
I mean, if I love him, and I'm in Hell,
Since he loves me, he must be there as well!
The Bible says: "Love keeps no score of wrongs",
And it's with Isabelle that he belongs...
Yes! I forgive him!

(a pious simper gives way to a scowl, and she reproaches herself)

        Lyse! What's wrong with you?
Vengeance is mine. That's in the Bible, too!
He loves you, and he leaves you on the rocks –
You love him, and you're made a laughing stock!
If it was love that got you in this state,
What's going to get you out of it but hate?
When love turns sour, it brings its own rewards:
Revenge tastes even sweeter afterwards!
(Exit, cackling)

(ACT III; PP 99-100)

The Sisterhood
(LES FEMMES SAVANTES)

MOLIERE 1672
translated & adapted by Ranjit Bolt 1987

Armande and Henriette are sisters. Armande is anti-marriage and
anti-men and, like their mother, thinks one should devote one's life
to literature. Henriette is in love with Clitandre, so argues:

'People are different — some of us are blessed
With aspirations and a brilliant mind —
Others are less ... platonically inclined:
I can't reverse the accident of birth
That made you lofty, and me down-to-earth'.

ARMANDE

"Marriage" — think back: when have you ever heard
Such a supremely nauseating word?
A word that made you feel so out of sorts?
A word that conjured up such ghastly thoughts?
Why aren't you shuddering? Do you realise
What living torment such a word implies?

I'm horrified to see you've sunk this low!
Have you so little sense of your potential
That you believe such trivia essential?
Does happiness mean nothing better than
Spawning some brats and worshipping a man?
Is that your view? Of course not — it's absurd.
Please, leave such "pleasures" to the common herd,
And while they wallow in them, set your sights
On higher things and more refined delights.
To join our sisterhood you must reject
The sensory world and trust the intellect.

Just look at Mother: many feel that she

Deserves a place in the Académie,
And Monsieur Trissotin is in no doubt
That anti-feminists have kept her out.
How else can either of us justify
Being *her* daughter than by aiming high?
Marriage is slavery, but it needn't be —
Not if ... literature and philosophy
Are what you marry — sociology
Politics, semantics, semiology,
Hermeneutics, logic — disciplines like these
Won't beat you up or screw their secretaries —
These are my husbands — frankly, I'm appalled
By all this hankering after love, so-called.

(ACT I; PP 76-77)

The School for Wives
(L'ECOLE DES FEMMES)

MOLIERE 1662
translated & adapted by Neil Bartlett 1990

Agnes' guardian is Arnold, who has been over-protective since she was
a baby. Now that she has matured, Arnold plans to marry her. He keeps
her locked up while he is away from town; she waits by the window
for him. She is simple, naive, with no experience of life. She has no
idea of Arnold's intentions towards her, so tells him her 'strange story'.

AGNES

I was by the window, the light's good for working,
When I saw this young man, very handsome, walking,
Under the trees, and when he looked up and saw me
First he smiled and then he waved very politely
And I remembered how you always used to tell
Me I should be polite, so then I waved as well.
Suddenly, he waved again with a great big smile
So of course I waved back to him for a short while;
And then when he gave me his next wave, number three,
Of course by then I knew what he wanted from me.
I waved back. Then he went, and came back, and ev'ry
Time he came back he waved so very politely;
And I was watching him, closely, all of the time,
And ev'ry time he waved I gave him one of mine.
If it hadn't got dark I'd have stayed there for hours
And in fact, I'd still be at that window of ours,
'Cause I couldn't bear it, if I'd left, he'd have thought
That I didn't have as good manners as I ought.

The next day, I opened the door, but instead
Of him was a woman, standing there, and she said
"You are a lucky girl, God bless you, and keep you.
And may you always look as lovely as you do."

(she thinks about this)
Then she said, "When God makes a person beautiful
He doesn't do it so that they can hurt people.
But you have hurt someone; someone's heart is in pain
Because of you, and he has sent me to complain."
Me? I've *hurt* somebody? I cried out, astonished.
Yes, she said, you've hurt him, and you don't even know
And it's him you saw yesterday from your window.
Oh no! I said, but how? But what did I do wrong?
Did he get in trouble 'cause I kept him so long?
Oh, I didn't mean it! It was your eyes, she said.
It was the way you looked that has left him half dead.
Oh God! I said, I had to, such was my surprise,
How could my eyes do that? What is wrong with my eyes?
Oh, she said, don't you know; looking is dangerous;
And eyes like yours can be 'specially contagious;
And in fact he's so sick that he's losing his mind
And if you can't, she said – she was just being kind –
Find it in your hard heart to help him in some way
Then your young man will go mad and die by Tuesday.
Oh God I said, that would make me so unhappy.
I'll help him get better, what does he want from me?
All that he wants, she said, all that he wants to do
Is to see you again, alone; to talk to you.
Only your eyes can stop him getting any worse;
You have infected him; now you can be his nurse.
Oh! Oh! I said – I had to say – If he's that sick
Tell him to come whenever he wants. Fetch him! Quick.

So he came. And saw me. And I made him better.
(justifying herself to Arnold)
I thought of what you'd think when deciding whether
To do it – how could I have endured my consience
If he suffered and died without my assistance? –
I can't bear it, seeing people suffer –
I even had to cry when my dog was run over.

(ACT II; PP 142-143)

Le Misanthrope

MOLIERE 1666
translated & adapted by Neil Bartlett 1988

Celimene's hosting an eventful at–home party. It's late at night, and
Arsinoe arrives uninvited. There is little love lost between them.
Celimene says of her:

>*'I know the Bitch is a Nun*
>*But what she really wants, beneath that 'modest' dress,*
>*Is to pick someone up'.*

Arsinoe tells Celimene all the gossip she has heard about her; and so
Celimene returns the compliment.

CELIMENE

Madame, I'm deeply indebted to your good sense;
And to repay the debt, to show there's no offence,
I feel that now I must, without hesitation,
Share some news that touches on your reputation.
And since you've proved the quality of your friendship
By relaying back to me all the foul gossip
You have heard about me, I'd like to do the same,
And repeat the slanders I've heard to blacken your name.

The other day I too had lunch with some people
Whose moral standards are absolutely model.
We discussed, at lunch, as these days one does tend to do,
Popular morality. Someone mentioned you.
Your prudishness, your hysterical piety
Were *not* considered to be exemplarary.
The way that you contrive to look so very clean,
Your speeches about intellectual hygiene,
Your strange obsession with finding things indecent,
The way you find filth even in the innocent,
The very high regard which you have for your own self
The clear contempt with which you look down from the

shelf.
Your relentless sermonising and the shrill, mean
Tone with which you condemn ordinary good clean
Fun; all these features – since we're friends I feel able
To tell you this – were condemned by the whole table.
What's the use, we all said, of an exterior
That looks good, if there's rot in the interior?
She believes in prare, ev'ry Sunday she says them,
But she abuses her staff and underpays them,
She talks a lot about the cost of vanity
But she certainly looks like she's made up to me.
She proclaims that pornography is disgusting;
But she certainly has a taste for the real thing,
Well I defended you, and said there must be under
Some delusion to credit such vulgar slander,
But nothing that I said could change their opin'on;
They said – referring to you I suppose – that one
Should take a bit more int'rest in one's own affairs
And take just a little less interest in theirs;
That one's own personal life should be scrutinised
Hard and Long before another's is criticised;
That there are some standards to which one must conform
Before one talks t'others about moral reform;
And that, actually, the job is better done
By those who make preaching their full-time profeshun.

Madame, you are I know too clever a woman
Not to take advice in the spirit it's given.
And won't suspect any base motive that's not there;
I am motivated only by your welfare.

(ACT III; PP 93-94)

Bérénice

RACINE 1670
translated & adapted by Neil Bartlett 1990

Bérénice, Queen of Palestine, is to marry Titus. But now that he is
the new Emperor of Rome, Titus is torn between private desire and
public duty – Rome does not want a Queen. He has been avoiding
making a decision one way or another, much to Rome's and
Bérénice's frustration.

BERENICE

I know I'm being rude, please do not be angry,
I know I'm intruding upon your privacy.
While the whole of your court surrounds me and stuns me
With the noise of honours that you have just done me,
Is it fair that, my Lord, I alone seem not to
Be given a hearing, to voice my thanks to you?
But, my Lord (I assume that your adviser here
'S privy to our secrets and to all we hold dear)
Your mourning is over, nothing is stopping you,
You are alone, and you could come, don't you want to?
I *hear* you've offered me new lands of which I'm queen;
But you yourself cannot be heard, cannot be seen.
Alas, a bit less in State, Sir, more in private!
Can you only make love when you're in the Senate?
Ah! Titus, since Love's no respecter of persons
Or protocol, or rank, or official reasons,
Why should your love express itself so formally?
Are states all it has left that it wants to give me?
Since when did you think that I care about kingships?
Just one sigh, just one look, just one word from your lips;
That's what a heart like mine spends all its time wanting.
If you saw me sometimes you could give me nothing.
Does the Empire demand each minute of each day?
Your heart, after a week, has it nothing to say?

One word and I'd feel so much less scared than I do!
Were you discussing me when I burst in on you?
Am I what you discuss when you talk privately,
My Lord? Tell me you were at least thinking of me!

(ACT II, SCENE IV; PP 30-31)

The Eighteenth Century

Marivaux wrote challenging roles for leading *commedia dell'arte* performers at Paris' *Comédie-Italienne,* taking the performers beyond their skilled improvisation into dialogue of psychological complexity. Many of the roles were written for specific actors – such as all the Silvia roles, played by the leading lady of that name. His plays may seem like frothy love intrigues, but his concern for narrative is with its subtextual subtlety. We play roles as a way of discovering emotional truth: the way we communicate, rather than the fact that we communicate, being paramount. Like Alfred de Musset a century later (a playwright greatly influenced by Marivaux) he picked up on the nuances and dynamic interplay of language from the *salons* which he frequented in fashionable Paris society.

Meanwhile, Goldoni was reforming, reinventing *commedia* in Venice. His *riforma* threw off the masks and fleshed out the stock characters and pat plots, refined the coarseness of *commedia,* and introduced motivation. Thus a character like Mirandolina is sexually, socially and financially independent. Where Goldoni's writing is bold and brassy, Marivaux's peels away layers of gossamer.

In Lessing's studies in theatre criticism, *The Hamburg Dramaturgy* (1767), he argues that the highly-charged emotions of *sturm und drang* can take place in a bourgeois drama just as much as in a play set in the past with kings and mythological figures as its protagonists. He had proved this on the stage over a decade earlier with *Miss Sara Sampson*, the first time German theatre had seen a prose tragedy taken from contemporary life.

The Game of Love and Chance
(LE JEU DE L'AMOUR ET DU HASARD)

PIERRE MARIVAUX 1730
translated & adapted by Neil Bartlett 1992

Silvia, A Society Woman, is chastising her maid Lisette for telling
Silvia's father that Silvia is keen to be married. Lisette tries to
persuade her mistress that the man her father has picked is: 'Practical
and Decorative; he's got the lot'. Silvia is not convinced – 'I am not
bored with being single' – and anyway, she doesn't want to marry
any old Tom, Dick, or Harry...

SILVIA

In marriage, one requires the reasonable, not the desirable.
Actually, all I'm looking for is decency, and that's harder to
find in a man than people think. This one comes highly
recommended; but I don't know anyone who's actually
sampled the goods. Men are so prone to making false claims
about themselves. Especially the clever ones. And I should
know, knowing as I do the most eligible men in town. It's
all so charming, so very reasonable, so very amusing, they all
look as smart as indeed one finds they are. "He looks a
decent sort, such a dependable, solid sort," one used to hear
that all the time about Tom. "Well he is," people used to
say. I myself used to say. "What you see is what you get
with Tom." Oh yes, there's a face one can trust, so
charming, so considerate, so easily transformed a quarter of
an hour later into that of an aggressive boor who terrorises
an entire household. Tom got married; and now that's all his
wife, his children and his staff ever see of him, while he still
goes about Town parading the friendly physiognomy by
which we all recognise him and which is in fact nothing but
a mask he puts on with his hat whenever he leaves the
house.

And doesn't everyone take one look at Dick and instinctively adore him? Well, in the privacy of his own home the man never utters a word, never laughs, never even lets slip a sigh; he's not so much incommunicative as inert; ice, inside. His own wife has no idea what's going on in his head; they never talk; she's married to a kind of frigid recluse who only ever leaves his study to come down to dinner – at which he then makes the whole table simply die of depression, chilliness and boredom. What fun that must be.

What about that Harry. The other day they had had some sort of row; I called; I was announced, and I watched him come down to greet me with open arms, charm itself; from the way he was smiling one would have thought I had merely interrupted some quite inconsequential conversation. The beast. That's what men are like. One would never have known that his wife was in tears. Over him. I found her in a complete state, white as a sheet, eyes ruined with all that weeping. I found her in the sort of state in which I may one day find myself. I recognised my future self in that portrait, my probable destiny as a cheap reproduction. I felt sorry for her, Lisette; imagine, one day, you may feel sorry for me. What an appalling idea.

So there you have him. "The Husband." What do you think?

(ACT I, SCENE I; PP 13-14)

Successful Strategies
(L'HEUREUX STRATAGEME)

MARIVAUX 1733
translated by Timberlake Wertenbaker 1983

La Comtesse was in love with, and betrothed to, Dorante.
However, she has been enjoying the attentions of Le Chevalier
Damis. Lisette, her maid, is trying to find out where her true
affections lie, but La Comtesse is determined to follow the
fluctuations of her heart. Lisette says: 'What a fickle heart you have.
You have so much sense, how can you be unfaithful? Because that's
what people will say'. La Comtesse replies.

COMTESSE

Do you think you frighten me with that big word?
Unfaithful! These words are used to intimidate the faint-
hearted. They're given weight but when you think about
them, they're worthless.

This heart, when it gives its word and breaks it, time and
time again, is only following its call. It goes wherever its
changing impulses carry it, and cannot do otherwise. What's
all this nonsense? Far from calling unfaithfulness a crime, I
maintain that, if tempted, one musn't hesitate for an instant.
Otherwise, you're deceiving people, and that must be
avoided at all costs.

Dorante has charming notions. Am I, just because he loves
me, never to dare cast a look elsewhere? Is he the only one
who has a right to find me young and lovely? Must I seem a
hundred years old to everyone else and bury all my
attractions? Am I to devote my whole life to the sad sterility
of pleasing only him? Oh, no doubt. That's how these
gentlemen want us to live. According to them, there must
be only one man and he must compose your entire

universe. All the others are debarred, they might as well be dead. Too bad if your self-regard isn't satisfied and you sometimes wish for these others. Faithfulness, stupid faithfulness has ordained that you must be content with only one captive. Resign yourself and bear with it. What oppression, Lisette, what oppression. Go, go and talk to Dorante, forget your reservations. Do you think men go to such lengths when they want to leave us? Doesn't every day bring new proof of their inconstancy? Do they have privileges we're not allowed to enjoy? You must be joking. The Chevalier loves me, I don't dislike him. I won't do any violence to my inclinations.

(ACT I, SCENE IV; PP 84-85)

Mirandolina
(LA LOCANDIERA)

CARLO GOLDONI 1753
translated by Ranjit Bolt 1993

Mirandolina has inherited her father's business: 'a young girl, trying
to run an inn by herself. It's tough'. She's not without many offers of
help – the rich Count Albafiorita and the poor Marquess of Forlipopoli
are both in love with her, as are all the men who stay at her inn
(except Ripafratta, who hates women). The Marquess says that if he
wasn't of such high rank then 'dammit, I'd marry you!'. She's spunky.

MIRANDOLINA

Charming! "Demmit, I'd marry you"! Who does he think
he is? Imagine being his wife. (I like to eat now and then,
for a start.)

God knows, if I'd married everyone who wanted me, there'd
be a husband in every room by now. I'm lovely – and they
love me. What can I do? They pay the bill, they propose, I
send them packing. It's practically a daily occurrence. That
oaf Ripafratta's about the first one who hasn't gone gooey-
eyed at the sight of me ... Well, perhaps I'm exaggerating.
But it is rather irritating, all the same. He hates women, does
he? Why? What's wrong with him? Nothing I can't fix, at
any rate! I like a challenge. It's a weakness of mine, you see: I
have to make everyone adore me. I thrive on it. And the
count? He'll have to look elsewhere. Money has its uses, of
course – but it's not everything. It's not as if you can't be
independent and respectable at the same time. Besides, I've
got a mission: to convince the doubters that women really are
the best idea Nature ever came up with.

(ACT I, SCENE I; P 113)

Sara
(MISS SARA SAMPSON)

GOTTHOLD LESSING 1755
translated by Ernest Bell

Sara Sampson has eloped with her lover Mellefont. They have
been staying in an inn for nine weeks. It hasn't been a happy time for
Sara because she is desperate for Mellefont to marry her and make an
honest woman of her. Her ever kind father discovers where she is
hiding and sends his manservant, Waitwell, with a letter containing
'love and forgiveness'. She refuses to read it, saying that she must
have made her father most unhappy.

SARA

To grieve a father such as he, this I have had the courage
to do. But to see him forced by this very grief – by his love
which I have forfeited, to look with leniency on all the
wrong into which an unfortunate passion has led me; this,
Waitwell, I could not bear. If his letter contained all the
hard and angry words which an exasperated father can utter
in such a case, I should read it – with a shudder it is true –
but still I should be able to read it. I should be able to
produce a shadow of defence against his wrath, to make him
by this defence if possible more angry still. My consolation
then would be this – that melancholy grief could have no
place with violent wrath and that the latter would transform
itself finally into bitter contempt. And we grieve no more
for one whom we despise. My father would have grown
calm again, and I would not have to reproach myself with
having made him unhappy for ever. His yearning for me
misleads him, perhaps, to give his consent to everything.
But no sooner would this desire be appeased a little, than he
would feel ashamed before himself of his weakness. Sullen
anger would take possession of him, and he would never be
able to look at me without silently accusing me of all that I

had dared to exact from him. Yes, if it were in my power to
spare him his bitterest grief, when on my account he is
laying the greatest restraint upon himself: if at a moment
when he would grant me everything I could sacrifice all to
him; then it would be quite a different matter. I would take
the letter from your hands with pleasure, would admire in it
the strength of the fatherly love, and, not to abuse this love,
I would throw myself at his feet a repentant and obedient
daughter. But can I do that? I shall be obliged to make use
of his permission, regardless of the price this permission has
cost him. And then, when I feel most happy, it will
suddenly occur to me that he only outwardly appears to
share my happiness and that inwardly he is sighing – in
short, that he has made me happy by the renunciation of his
own happiness. And to wish to be happy in this way, – do
you expect that of me, Waitwell? There is no answer to it.
So take your letter back! If my father must be unhappy
through me, I will myself remain unhappy also. To be quite
alone in unhappiness is that for which I now pray Heaven
every hour, but to be quite alone in my happiness – of that I
will not hear.

(Act III, Scene iii; pp 45-46)

Sara
(MISS SARA SAMPSON)

GOTTHOLD LESSING 1755
translated by Ernest Bell

Marwood is the embittered ex-lover of Mellefont, with whom she had a daughter, Arabella. Mellefont's passions are now centred on the young Sara Sampson. Marwood feverishly hatches plots to divide the two: 'If his heart should be deaf to an old love, the language of blood will at least be audible to him'...

MARWOOD

Ha! Now I see what it is that makes you so perverse. Well, I will lose no more words. Be it so! Be assured I shall do everything to forget you. And the first thing that I will do to this end, shall be this. You will understand me! Tremble for your Bella! Her life shall not carry the memory of my despised love down to posterity; my cruelty shall do it. Behold in me a new Medea! Or, if you know a more cruel mother still, behold her cruelty doubled in me! Poison and dagger shall avenge me. But no, poison and dagger are tools too merciful for me! They would kill your child and mine too soon. I will not see it dead. I will see it dying! I will see each feature of the face which she has from you disfigured, distorted, and obliterated by slow torture. With eager hand will I part limb from limb, vein from vein, nerve from nerve, and will not cease to cut and burn the very smallest of them, even when there is nothing remaining but a senseless carcass! I – I shall at least feel in it – how sweet is revenge!

My ravings are not directed against the right person. The father must go first! He must already be in yonder world, when, through a thousand woes the spirit of his daughter follows him. *(she advances towards* Mellefont *with a dagger which she draws from her bosom)* So die, traitor!

(ACT II, SCENE VII; P 37)

The Nineteenth Century

Aleksander Fredro is hardly known in Europe at all, and yet he is 'the Father of Polish Comedy'. The comedy is a mischievous satire: of society, of social ills, of *nouveau riches* socialites. His attitude to women is interesting: his translator, Noel Clark, observes that the plays 'reflect the author's awareness of the disabilities suffered by young women in a male-dominated society' – though he 'remains ambivalent', says Clark. In the mid 19th century, Fredro's plays were welcomed as home-grown drama in a theatre dominated by the classical comedies of France (Molière) and Italy (Goldoni). While Fredro owes something to these playwrights, he also looks forward to the satirical plays of Russia (Ostrovsky).

Unusually for 19th century plays, Fredro's comedies are in rhyming verse – this was the century of prose naturalism, which found its most comfortable home in the novel. Yet the Spanish playwright, Zorrilla, also plays with rhyme in *The Real Don Juan*. While we may be most familiar with the infamous rake Don Juan through Mozart's opera *Don Giovanni,* his legend is best known in Spanish popular culture through Zorrilla's play. (His first incarnation on stage was in Tirso de Molina's Spanish Golden Age classic *The Last Days of Don Juan*.)

Alfred de Musset was a poet as well as a playwright, and his plays are as lyrical as they they are graceful and witty. But these surface qualities – like the best work of the 18th century playwright Marivaux – reveal a deeper psychological insight when his characters bare their vexed souls. De Musset's plays were first performed as readings in the fashionable *salons* he frequented. There he would have experienced subtextual anxiety lurking beneath surface propriety. They were only later performed on stage, when he regained the confidence to suffer public scrutiny after the failure of an early play. As much as de Musset's work is based on observation, it is also rooted in his personal life: from 1833-1835, he was involved in a tempestuous affair with George Sand (the *nom de plume* of the successful novelist Aurore Duoin – her private life was notorious; amongst her lovers was the pianist and composer Chopin). It is within this broad context that one can appreciate de Musset's curiously pleasing mix of potty scenarios, uncannily modern sensitivities, and subtle passion.

Nick Dear's wicked version of Ostrovsky's *A Family Affair* for Cheek by Jowl was not just a huge success because of a boisterous, leering production, but because it also scurrilously captured the spirit of late 1980's selfish decadence. Dear freely adapted the play: 'I have tried to make new jokes where the old ones weren't funny, and new plot where the old one chugged up a strange Muscovite siding of its own'. It was Ostrovsky's first full-length play and was immediately banned by order of Tsar Nicholas I because of its searing exposé of disorder amongst the merchant classes.

Zola was a novelist of the Naturalist school. The story of *Thérèse Raquin* was taken from a newspaper article, conceived as a novel, and then adapted for the stage by Zola himself. Pip Broughton (the translator of his stage version) says that 'the play flourishes in the truthful portrayal of huge passions: lust, greed, terror'; and she adds: 'a huge intensity of playing and courage is required of the actors to make the text live'.

The great Russian novelist Tolstoy wrote the play *The Power of Darkness* in 1886, but it was not performed until 1895, and then only with a revised Act IV. Tolstoy's quest to educate the Russian people in morality repulsed the Holy Synod. Tsar Alexander III, who initially thought it a wonderful play, later claimed (after the Holy Synod's complaints) that 'the play cannot be performed because it is too realistic and its subject matter too horrible'.

Virgins Vows
(SLUBY PANIENSKIE)

ALEKSANDER FREDRO 1832
translated by Noel Clark 1987

Clara is staying with her cousin Aniela in the country. Despite
'country living's rich monotony', they have made a vow not to dally
with the insincere love of men. Clara, 'a merry spark', resists the suits
of melancholic Albin, 'misery incarnate'. Clara believes:

'Of all adventures, love's the very worst;
In case of danger, opt for drowning first!'.

Clara debates Albin's advances, and those of men in general, with
Aniela.

CLARA

No! Let the idiot love, weep, groan and – perish!
Fie on his love so-called! Freedom I cherish!

      Am I to face him, curtsey thrice?
Twisting my apron blushing lobster-red
And, stammering in an effort to be nice,
Expect him meekly to accept the fact
That I reject him, as I do all creatures male?

Tact wouldn't work! He'd take it in his stride:
Man's heart is made of sterner stuff by far!
Each wound is swiftly hidden by a scar –
A scar which then becomes his badge of pride!
Male vanity is proof against all blows:
The more you punish it, the more it grows!
Scold them, despise them, hate them – all no use!
Men thrive on anger, loathing and abuse...
Until some poor unfortunate (not us),
Patience exhausted, worn out by the fuss,
So battle-weary that her wits elude her,

Succumbs to love for *peace* from the intruder!

Women's virtue isn't in dispute.
Women were good but what did that achieve?
Men had their fun; women were left to grieve!

(mounting vehemence)
Would you forgo revenge because one man
Grieves, having stalked in vain and lost his prize?
Determined not to wed, should we our plan,
By indiscreet rejection, publicise –
Destroying hope for one and all thereby,
Sparing the self-esteem of would-be swains?
Certainly not! We'll none of that, say I!
You who do boast your victory in love's campaigns –
Down on your knees, men! Bend your haughty necks!
Suffer, each one, our scorn for all your sex!

(ACT I, SCENE I; PP 130-131)

A Door Must Be Kept Open Or Shut
(Il Faut Qu'une Porte Soit Ouverte Ou Fermee)

Alfred de Musset 1845
translated by Peter Meyer 1955

Paris: the **Marquise**, as is the fashion, is waiting to receive her
friends and acquaintances for blasé gossip. Her neighbour, the Baron,
has dropped by early. They bemoan at-homes and society balls, for
such a life can be languid and boring: 'I'm as dull as a three volume
novel,' protests the Baron: 'Perhaps we're just growing old. I'm
almost thirty and I'm losing my zest for life,' says the Marquise.
During his visit the Baron declares his love; she will have none of it.

THE MARQUISE

You think I'm beautiful, I imagine, and it amuses you to
tell me so. Well, what follows? What does that prove? Is
that any reason why I should love you? I take it that if I like
someone, it's not because I am beautiful. What's the point
of these compliments? You men think the way to make a
woman love you is to stand in front of her, look her up and
down through an eyeglass as if she was a dummy in a shop
window, and say to her very pleasantly, "Madame, I think
you're charming." Add a few hackneyed phrases and a
bouquet of flowers, and that's what you call paying court to
her.

Rubbish! How can an intelligent man enjoy such nonsense?
It puts me in a rage to think of it. You must imagine a
woman to be completely brainless, if you hope to succeed
with that kind of recipe. Do you think she finds it amusing
to pass her life listening to a perpetual flow of balderdash
and to have her ears filled with nonsense from morning to
night? Really, I think if I were a man and saw a pretty
woman, I'd say to myself, "Now there's a poor creature
who must be overwhelmed with compliments. I would

spare her, pity her, and if I wanted to try to please her, I'd do her the honour of speaking of something other than her wretched face. But no. Always: "You're beautiful" and then: "You're beautiful" and again: "Beautiful." Heavens, we know that. Do you need me to tell you that all you men of fashion are nothing but confectioners in disguise?

(P 124)

Don't Fool With Love
(ON NE BADINE PAS AVEC L'AMOUR)

ALFRED DE MUSSET 1834
translated & adapted by Declan Donnellan 1993

Camille, a 'glorious flower of wisdom and devotion', has been
educated in a nunnery for ten years. Her uncle, her ward, summons
her to return home when she comes of age (eighteen) since she can
now inherit the estate her mother bequeathed her. Her uncle also
plans for his son Perdican, recently returned from university, to marry
Camille. But virginal zeal has been impressed upon Camille by the
nuns' experiences of men, much to Perdican's disdain. Camille protests
that she is right to renounce marriage and become a Bride of Christ.

CAMILLE

I had a friend who was a nun. She was only thirty years old,
and had an income of five hundred thousand pounds at the
age of fifteen. She was the most beautiful creature who ever
walked on earth. She was a peeress, married to one of the
most distinguished men in France. She possessed all the gifts
nature could bestow. And like a healthy sapling, each of her
buds bore shoots. Never did love and happiness garland a
nobler brow. Her husband deceived her; she fell for another
man. She died in despair.

We shared the same cell. And many a night I'd spend
talking to her about her misfortunes. Her sorrows became
mine. That's strange, isn't it? I don't know how that
happened. She spoke to me often about her marriage; how
the first months of frenzied pleasure gave way to serene joy.
Then how she would sit of an evening by the fire, and he
would lean on the window, without their exchanging a
single word. How their love languished, and how every
effort at starting afresh ended in quarrels. How love-affairs
started to divide them and slide in and out of their suffering.

I could see all this happening, and lived her story as she told it. When she used to say, "Then I was happy", my heart leapt; and when she added, "Then I was sad", I cried. My tears fell. And do you know something even more singular? In the end I created for myself an imaginary life. It lasted for four years. It's impossible to tell you how this happened. But what I must tell you, is that through all her stories and all the inventions of my dreams, I could make out your features. But that's quite natural. You were the only man I'd ever known. And in all truth, I did love you, Perdican.

There are two hundred women in our convent. A few have never known life. The rest are waiting for death. Many leave the convent as I have, virgins, and full of hope. These return shortly afterwards, old and desolate. They all die on their horsehair mattresses. And younger ones take their place. Visitors always admire the calm and order of the house. They stare at the deep white of our veils. We lower our eyes to meet their stare. What do you think about these women, Perdican? Were they right or were they wrong?

Some have urged me to remain a virgin. It would be nice to be able to ask your advice. Would those women have been better off to take a lover, and would you advise me to do the same?

My mind is full of ideas and some of them are absurd and ridiculous. Probably I haven't learnt properly. I'm just repeating like a parrot. In the gallery there's a little picture of a monk bent over his missal; through the dark bars of his cell slides a weak beam of light and in the distance one can make out an Italian gondolier dancing in the sunshine. Which of those men do you respect the more?

I want to love, but I don't want to suffer. I want to love with an eternal love, and make vows which cannot be broken. Here is my lover. *(She shows him her crucifix.)*
(ACT II, SCENE V; PP 36-38)

The Real Don Juan
(DON JUAN TENORIO)

JOSÉ ZORRILLA 1844
translated & adapted by Ranjit Bolt 1990

Don Juan has a wager with his old rival, Don Luis, that he can bed
Dona Ines and Dona Ana (Don Luis' betrothed) in one night – or
die. Having already plotted how to get Dona Ana, Don Juan has
instructed Ines' nurse, **Brigida,** to help him. Brigida has obviously
played her part well:
> *'Oh, she's primed alright!*
> *Don't worry – she'll be putty in your hands.'*

BRIGIDA

    Look: she understands
Nothing of life – she's like a lovely bird
That's been imprisoned in its cage since birth –
Hopping about – not having seen the sky
It doesn't have the slightest urge to fly –
Or show its feathers off to anyone,
Not having seen them glitter in the sun.
Poor little thing! She's barely seventeen;
What would she know of love? She's never been
Outside the convent ... convent! Huh! Con*vict*
Is what she is – her training's been that strict.
The same old round, from one year to the next –
Confession, chapel, prayers, some holy text
Or other...

           I've filled her head with thoughts of you.
It's like I say – so far as she's concerned,
You're just the thing for which she's always yearned –
Unconsciously – if that's the word I want:
You're witty, worldy, handsome, brave, galant –
That's what I told her – I believed it, too!

Of course, I also had to tell some lies.
        That you were suffering agonies
Of love for her – that if the situation
Went on, your life, or worse, your reputation
Might be at risk – I even said you were
Her father's choice! In short, I peppered her
With such a host of clever arguments,
She's set her heart on you – her innocence
Is fading fast!

                As soon as compline starts to chime –
You make your move – you're going to have to climb
A wall or two – the rest of it should be
Extremely easy – simply take the key
I gave that servant, and unlock the gate –
You'll find a narrow passage, leading straight
To us.
        I'll stop off at the gate –
Talk to the porter – put her off the scent.
I'll see you later.

(ACT II; PP 40-41)

The Real Don Juan
(DON JUAN TENORIO)

JOSÉ ZORRILLA 1844
translated & adapted by Ranjit Bolt 1990

The **Abbess** looks after Ines in the convent. Ines is strangely
troubled this evening and the Abbess is trying to comfort her.

The convent. Dona Ines' *cell.*

ABBESS

You're young and beautiful – but virtuous;
You've spent your whole life, almost, here with us:
To enter holy vows, no evidence
Of your commitment – acts of penitence,
Or other trials – are needed: how can one
Repent the wicked things one hasn't done?!
Renounce a world one's hardly even seen?
You see how blessed your situation's been!

    No earthly pleasures or emotions
Can haunt your dreams and trouble your devotions:
How happy is the novice who recalls
No bustling world beyond the convent walls –
A tender dove, obedient to command,
Fearlessly feeding from her master's hand –
A little garden bounds her wish and care,
Nor does she try the nets that keep her there,
Or gaze, with longing, at the upper air –
No: like a lily in God's loveliest glade,
Your petals opened here, and here they'll fade.
Such innocence, once lost, will not return –
Hold fast to it! But why so taciturn?
So sullen? This is not like you ... Of course!
You're always lost without that nurse of yours ...

I'll send her here – she should be back by now –
She went to see your father. Anyhow
It's time you were in bed – goodnight, my dear.

(ACT III; P 45)

The Real Don Juan
(DON JUAN TENORIO)

JOSÉ ZORRILLA 1844
translated & adapted by Ranjit Bolt 1990

Ines has been whisked away from the safety of her convent to Don
Juan's estate, where he is to claim her honour as part of a wager.
Ines' nurse, who has helped to plot Don Juan's night of passion,
primed Ines with high praises of Don Juan – so much so that Ines has
already begun to fall for him. Now that he confronts her in the flesh,
she is unable to resist.

INES

I've never known such agony before!
It's killing me! For pity's sake, no more!
Fire in my heart and throbbing in my brain!
You say you love me, yet you cause me pain!
What secret potion have you given me,
To undermine a virgin's modesty?
What magic amulet do you possess
Whose force is drawing me to your caress?
Satan himself had charm – and beauty, too –
What he denied God, has he granted you?
Your power's too great – there's no resisting it –
My will is being eroded, bit by bit!
Look how the river's sucked into the sea –
Such is the influence you exert on me;
Your presence thrills me and destroys my reason;
Your eyes bewitch my soul – your breath is poison.
Be noble – show compassion: since I burn
With love, kill me! Or love me in return.

(melting) Yours for eternity!

(ACT IV; P 59)

A Family Affair
(Svoi Lyudi – Sochtsemsya!)

Ostrovsky 1850
adapted by Nick Dear 1988

Lipochka's a spoilt, overgrown adolescent who scoffs meringues and trifle, and is desparate to marry above her station. Her social climbing fantasies are rudely cut down to size by her soon-to-be bankrupt merchant father (Bolshov) and *petit bourgeois* mother. (She's the first person we meet.)

Bolshov's *house*.

LIPOCHKA

I love dancing. The new dances. I love them. There is nothing in the world more exciting than going dancing. You drive off to a do at the Assembly Rooms, say, or to someone's wedding, you're simply dripping scent and hothouse flowers, you're dressed up like a drawing in a fashion magazine. Or a toy. A man's toy. You sit prettily. You feign disinterest in the proceedings. Inside ten seconds some young fellow's materialised at your shoulder and he mutters, "May I have the pleasure of this dance?". The pleasure of this dance ... If he looks as if he can tell funny stories, or better still if he's an army man, you lower your eyelids fractionally and reply, "Why yes you may". Never take students, poets, or clerks. Stick out for an army man. With a great big sword. And a moustache. And epaulettes. And tiny little bells on his spurs going tinkle-tinkle, tinkle-tinkle as he strides across the room. Ooh ... ! The sound of a young colonel as he buckles on his sword! Like thunder crackling in my heart. I want a military man. I don't want a pudding in a dull civilian suit. I'd sooner die.

Most women at dances sit in the corners with their doughy

old legs crossed. Can't think why. It's such fun! It's not
difficult. At first I was a bit embarrassed in front of my tutor
– a Frenchman actually – but after twenty lessons I
understood everything perfectly. I learn quick. The other
girls don't, because they are dimwitted, superstitious, and
lacking the beneficiaries of a decent education. My dancing-
master touches my knees. Mama gets horribly angry. But he
has to do it. It's part of the course.

(strange faraway look) I was just having a vision just then. An
officer in the Imperial Guard has proposed to me. We are
celebrating our engagement in the guard style. Shimmering
candles ... waiters in white gloves ... My dress is made of
tulle or gauze. A waltz strikes up. But I decline to dance.
My beau is disconcerted. I blush for shame. Perhaps he
suspects that I am unschooled! He asks me what's the
matter. What's the matter? What's the matter? *(shrieks)* I
haven't danced for a year and half, that's what's the matter!
I've forgotten the stupid steps!

(She practices, waltzing badly. She's in her underwear.)

(ACT I; PP 9-10)

A Family Affair
(SVOI LYUDI – SOCHTSEMSYA!)

OSTROVSKY 1850
adapted by Nick Dear 1988

Ustinya's a match-maker, a lucrative vocation in social climbing Moscow. Priding herself on being good at her job, she perseveres with awkward customers like the Bolshov family. She's spent all winter searching out an acceptable husband for their daughter, Lipochka. At last she's found a smallfry nobleman. But now Lazar, Samson Bolshov's assistant, wants her to persuade them to accept a merchant 'friend' (himself) instead. The offer of a sable coat in exchange for her efforts tempts her.

USTINYA

Well *actually* I have laid it on a bit thick – that this chap's rich, handsome, lovesick and so on ... When really he's ... But how am I to put Samson Bolshov off? You know stubborn he is. He'll chew me up and spit out the gristle.

So? How many aristocrats have pure blue blood? Nowadays every pretty girl in pigtails aspires to be a duchess. Take our Lipochka for example. She acts as if she was high-born, doesn't she, but not to put too fine a point on it, Lazar, her origins are worse than mine and, very possibly, yours. Her father used to trade in leather mittens – without linings! – on the Balchug. People called him Slippery Sam Bolshov and beat the daylight out of him whenever they got the opportunity. The old girl – Agrafena – is herself barely a cut above peasant stock. He plucked her from some mud-hut village, they scraped a few roubles together, and before you know it they've slithered into the middle class. So the daughter thinks she's practically bloody royal! It's only money. She's no better than me really. As for her upbringing – heaven preserve us. Her handwriting looks like an elephant jumped in the inkpot and then crawled round the page on its belly. Her French is execrable. And have you *seen* her dance?

(ACT II; P 45)

Thérèse Raquin

EMILE ZOLA 1865
translated by Pip Broughton 1983

Thérèse lives with her aunt/mother-in-law and cousin/husband,
weak Camille, above their haberdashers' shop in the dark, dank
Pont-Neuf Passage. She is released from her miserable existence by
the visits of Laurent, a colleague of Camille, whom she embraces as a
lover with uncontrollable passion (that is later to have catastrophic
consequences).

THERESE

Oh, what a childhood I had! I have been brought up in the
damp atmosphere of a sick man's room.

Oh yes! I was so miserable. For hours on end I would squat
in front of the fire stupidly watching over his infusions. If I
moved, my aunt scolded me – mustn't wake Camille up,
must we? I used to stammer; my hands shook like an old
woman's. I was so clumsy that even Camille made fun of
me. And yet I felt strong. I could feel my child's fists clench,
I wanted to smash everything ... They told me my mother
was the daughter of a nomadic African chief. It must be
true; so often I dreamt of escaping; roaming the roads and
running barefoot in the dust, begging like a gypsy ... you
see, I preferred starving in the wild to their hospitality. *(she
has raised her voice)*

I don't know why I ever agreed to marry Camille. It was a
pre-arranged marriage. My aunt simply waited until we
were of age. I was only twelve years old when she said,
"You will love your cousin, you will look after him." She
wanted him to have a nurse, an infusion-maker. She adored
this puny child that she had wrestled from death twenty
times, and she trained me to be his servant ... And I never

protested. They had made me cowardly. I felt pity for the child. When I played with him I could feel my fingers sink into his limbs like putty. On the evening of the wedding, instead of going to my room at the left on the top of the stairs, I went in Camille's, which was on the right. That was all ... But you ... you, my Laurent ... I love you. I loved you the day Camille pushed you into the shop, remember? I really don't know how I loved you. It was more like hate. The very sight of you drove me mad, I couldn't bear it. The moment you were there, my nerves were strained to breaking point, yet I waited achingly for you to come, for the pain. When you were painting just now, I was nailed to the stool, at your feet, no matter how hard I secretly tried to fight it.

And our only time of pleasure, Thursday evenings, when Grivet and old Michaud would arrive regular as clockwork, those Thursday evenings used to drive me mad – the eternal games of dominoes, eternal Thursdays, the same imbecilic boredom ... But now I feel proud and revenged. When we sit round the table exchanging polite remarks I can bask in such wicked pleasure; I sit there sowing and put on my half-baked expression while you all play dominoes; and in the midst of this bourgeois peace I'm reliving our moments of ecstacy.

(ACT I, SCENE V; PP 17-19)

The Power of Darkness

TOLSTOY 1886
translated & adapted by Anthony Clark 1984

Since **Anisya** poisoned her husband Piotr in order to marry his
young farm labourer Nikita, her life has been miserable. Nikita
squanders the inherited money on his affair with Akulina (Piotr's
daughter by his first marriage). Anisya believes that she'll win back
Nikita when Akulina is married off – but just before the wedding,
Akulina gives birth to Nikita's child. In a harrowing scene, the baby
is crushed to death and buried. Nikita becomes self-loathing and
even more distant from Anisya.

At Akulina's wedding, Anisya bravely, vainly hopes that the pain and
guilt of past misdeeds will be purged.

Enters, smartly dressed and flushed with drink.

ANISYA

Mother, it's going so well! Everybody's enjoying themselves.
Where is he?

... Look at him, he's all covered in straw! Had too much to
drink? *(laughs)* I'd like to cuddle up beside you ... Oh!
There isn't time! Come on, I'll show you the way. They're
all having such fun. It's lovely to see them enjoying
themselves. The concertina is playing away ... The women
are singing ... It's so beautiful. And everybody's drunk. It's
just as it should be.

It's so lively. People are already saying they've never known
a wedding like it. It's just as it should be. Come on, we'll go
together. I'm a bit tipsy, but I know the way.

(takes his arm)

What's the matter with you? You're so irritable. Our problems are over. We've got rid of the one thing that came between us. The girl is out of the way! We can enjoy ourselves. Like old times. Everything is going according to plan, and it's all legal. I can't tell you how happy I am. It's as if I was marrying you again! *(laughs)* Everybody's delighted. Everybody's grateful. They're all such wonderful people. There's old Ivan Moseich, and the policeman, singing our praises!

... I must get back. It must seem a bit strange ... as if the hosts have forgotten their guests. A bit rude, when the guests are such lovely people. Come on!

(ACT V, SCENE I; PP 84-85)

Early Modern Plays

Austria: Schnitzler was writing in Vienna at the same time as Freud; he explores the amorality of sexual adventures through his egocentric characters.

Norway: Ibsen's characters reveal their inner selves when affected by external forces, such as a volatile political situation or when they flout social conventions.

Sweden: Strindberg's philosophical chamber plays, written at the end of his life, have pared down characters almost stripped of their souls.

Italy: Pirandello uses theatrical allegories for the disintegration of society and the individual in contemporary Europe.

German Europe: Ödön von Horváth is concerned with the nature of the individual in a continent dehumanised by war. Writing his sequel to Beaumarchais' late 18th century Figaro Plays, he is preoccupied by the paradox of freedom in exile.

These playwrights dislocate themselves from the certainties of the past and explore a vision of the future. Their characters dream of being giants or are scared of being dwarfed.

Anatol

Arthur Schnitzler 1891
translated by Michael Robinson 1987

Anatol is rummaging through **Emilie**'s desk the night before their
wedding. Neither has a blameless past to say the least, yet Anatol is
wracked by hypocritical jealousy. Though they have made a pact to
destroy all the trinkets and memories of their numerous past affairs,
he discovers a ruby and a black diamond and demands that Emilie
explain these apparent love tokens: 'Admit it straight away, instead of
telling lies, like all the rest.'

EMILIE

Girls who can lie to you are lucky. No – you cannot bear
the truth! Just tell me one thing more: why have you always
begged me not to lie? 'I can forgive you anything except a
lie!' I can just hear you saying it now. And I – I – who told
you everything, abased myself, crawled in front of you,
shouted into your face 'Anatol, I'm a lost woman, but I love
you – !' I didn't use any of the stupid excuses that the others
always use. No, I told you the truth: Anatol, I have led a life
of pleasure, Anatol, I was lascivious, hot-blooded – I sold
myself, gave myself away – I am not worthy of your love.
Do you remember, I said all that before you even kissed my
hand? Yes, I wanted to run away from you because I loved
you so much, and you followed me – you begged for my
love – and I didn't want you, because I didn't want to sully
the man, who was more, who was different – well, was the
first man I loved. And then you took me, and I was yours.
How I shuddered, trembled, wept. And then you raised me
up so high, gave everything back to me again, piece by
piece, everything that they had taken from me – in your
impassioned arms I became what I had never been: pure –
and happy – you were so generous – you could forgive —.
And – now –

And now you're driving me away because I'm just like the rest after all.

(JEWELS AND MEMORIES; PP 49-50)

Rosmersholm

HENRIK IBSEN 1886
translated by David Rudkin 1990

Since the death of the parson John Rosmer's wife Beäta, her
companion **Rebecca** has been the parson's soulmate, sharing his life
withdrawn from society at Rosmersholm. As the town's political
turmoil brews, Rosmer decides to re-enter public life – not as a
conservative as his brother-in-law and those of his generation would
wish, but 'to raise all people in the land to a nobility'. This is the
Rosmer ethic. Rebecca is blamed for exerting too strong an
influence on Rosmer, scorned as 'an emancipated woman' by those
who equate 'free thinking' with 'free love'. When Rosmer asked her
to be his wife, she replied: 'I cannot go through life with a corpse on
my back' – which is not just the fear of being haunted by a former
wife, but an acknowledgement of the responsibility for Beäta's
suicide. Rebecca led Beäta 'to believe it her duty to make way' as 'a
childless wife'. Rebecca decides that she must now leave
Rosmersholm and return home.

REBECCA

Rosmersholm has reft me of my powers. Here has my brave
will been grounded. And maimed. That time's long gone
for me, when I had in me to venture anything. John
Rosmer, my capacity to do is lost. It has happened through
living with you. When at last I was alone with you here ...
and you were becoming your self ... Because you'd never
been wholly yourself, whilever Beäta was alive ... Once
though I was living with you here at last: quietly ... in
solitude ... and you were sharing your every, unreservèd
thought with me – each single emotion, be it so gentle or
delicate, as it came to you ... it's then the great change
happened. Little by little, you understand. Barely
perceivable ... but at last possessing all of me. To my deep
core. All that other... that ugly, drunken need, ebbed out so

far, so far from me. All those troubled urges in me, sank into
rest and were still. Over me there fell a peacefulness ... like
up at home there, that hush among a crag of seabirds at the
midnight sun.

It's all of it near said now, John. There remains only this,
that then a love came welling up in me. That great,
renunciating love, that is content with a share in living with
another: such as you and I have known. Yesterday ... when
you asked me, would I be your wife ... the jubilation cried
from me – for an instant. Of self-forgetting. Because that
was my easier will of old, all for pulling free again. But that
it has no power now ... none that's enduring.

It's Rosmer's morality ... or your morality, at least ... that
has blighted my will. And made it sick. Bound it in thrall to
a Commandment, that was of no weight with me before.
Through you ... living with you ... I am a nobler soul ...
You can be sure of it. The Rosmer ethic does make nobler
people of us. But ... *(shaking her head)* ... But it's death to
happiness, John.

(ACT IV; PP 158-160)

Thunder in the Air
(OVÄDER)

AUGUST STRINDBERG 1907
translated by Eivor Martinus 1988

Gerda returns with her daughter to the apartment block where she had lived with her husband – his brother tries to reunite them. He brings Gerda into the apartment where her ex-husband now lives with a new woman (with whom he now plays chess).

In the hallway

GERDA

(the clock chimes) Oh God! That chime ... I have carried it around with me for ten years now. This clock which never kept the time, but measured out the hours, the days and nights of five long years. *(looks around)* My piano ... and my plants ... the dining-table. He has looked after it well. It is polished like a shield. My sideboard with Eve and her knight in armour. Eve with her apples in the basket. And in the right-hand drawer, in the far corner there used to be a thermometer: *(pause)* I wonder if it is still there? Yes, there it is.

It became like a symbol of our relationship in the end. When we first got married the thermometer got left behind in this drawer. We meant to fix it outside the window and I promised to put it there, but then I forgot, and he promised to do it, but he forgot too, so we nagged each other about it and in the end I put it in this drawer in order to avoid further trouble. But I began to hate this thing and so did he. Do you realise what that meant? It meant that neither of us really believed in the permanence of our relationship. We revealed our true selves at once and didn't conceal our feelings of hostility. The first couple of months after we got

married we were ready to take a leap in the dark, always
prepared to break up. Like the themometer ... and here it is
still. Up and down, changeable like the weather. *(she puts
it aside and goes to the chessboard)* My chessboard ... which he
bought to pass the time while we were waiting for the baby
to arrive. Oh, that long wait. Who plays with him now?

(SCENE II; PP 35-36 –CHAMBER PLAYS PP 39-40)

The Pelican
(PELIKANEN)

AUGUST STRINDBERG 1907
translated by Eivor Martinus 1991

Gerda and her brother Frederik live in fear of their mother (the pelican of the title). Their father is dead. Frederik discovers a letter from their father explaining their mother's tyranny and how she is in league with Gerda's new husband. Though cold and starved, Gerda is fuelled by this letter to confront her mother.

GERDA

No, you gave me a bottle and stuck a dummy in my mouth. Then I had to go to the pantry and steal, but there was only rye bread which I had with mustard and when it burnt my throat I quenched my thirst with a bottle of spirit vinegar. The cruet stand and the bread basket, that was my larder.

(cries) I could forgive you everything, except that you took my life from me – yes, he was my life, because with him I started to live ... Don't say anything bad about father. I shall never be able to make up for what I've done to him, however long I live. But you're going to pay for it, because it was you who turned me against him. Do you remember when I was a little girl and you taught me to say awful hurtful things which I didn't understand. He was probably wise enough not to punish me for those arrows because he knew who'd shot them. Do you remember when you taught me to lie to him and say that I needed new books for school, and when you and I had cheated him out of money, we divided it up between us. How can I forget the past? Isn't there a draught that kills the memory without killing life? I wish I had the strength to leave everything behind, but like Frederik ... I'm powerless and weak ... we're your victims ... but you hardened creature can't even suffer for your own crimes.

(SCENE IV; PP 185-186)

The Black Glove
(SVARTA HANDSKEN)

AUGUST STRINDBERG 1907
translated by Eivor Martinus 1991

The **Young Wife** is rich and mean, vain and cruel, accusing her
maid of stealing a blue-stoned ring. The Christmas Spirit and
Christmas Fairy, of the apartment block where she lives, decide to
teach her a lesson, playing tricks on her – taking a black glove. They
also take her child away:

'She's not without a heart
it's just lacking in goodness, but sorrow will cure her'.

She is beside herself with grief, distraught and confused, and in a
kind of dream, she searches for her child throughout the building.

The Concierge*'s room.*

YOUNG WIFE
Where have I got to?
And where am I?
Where did I come from?
Who am I?
It must be a poor person living here ... but he's got so many
keys!
Is it a hotel?
No, a prison, an underground prison...
There shines the moon, it looks like a heart
and the clouds march past in black...
There's a forest, a forest of conifers,
a Christmas forest full of gifts and lights...
Inside the prison? No, this is some other place.
Anyone at home?

But wait! I remember, but the memory is behind...
and I went ahead to look for something.

What was I looking for?
A glove that I'd lost. It was black...
Now it's black again!
But I can see something blue in the dark,
like the sky in the spring ... appearing between white clouds,
a mountain lake between steep shores,
that's how blue my sapphire was ... that I lost...
the one they've stolen...
I've lost a few things these last few days...
I was cold and I was sitting in the dark...

It's warm but stuffy here;
the weight of the high tower at the top,
the heavy burden of human destinies,
I can feel them pressing me down, towards the earth...
pressing my heart in its weak rib-cage...
I wanted to speak but I couldn't find the words...
I wanted to cry as if I was grieving!

(catches sight of the boot)
What's this? A little boot?
A little stocking and a foot? In you go!
What was that? Here is a candle
that's sprouted branches, it's grown
from the root of the candlestick and soon
it will burst into flower,
three blue–white flowers with a bit of red inside...
I didn't know that candles could grow and sprout twigs.
Which part of the world have I got to?
An anchor buoy is floating in a forest here,
a wild boar's head is sticking up from the sea,
and the fish are walking on dry land.
(sees the print of the birth of Christ)
What's this? – A crib in a stable?
(starts to wake up)
And the shepherd's brown cows look with their big eyes,
at the little child ... who ... is asleep in the crib.
(wakes up and screams)

Oh Jesus Christ, save me!

I'm dying. I'm dying. — A child is born this night, a child
has died. There is the concierge ... he is angry with me
because I didn't give him a Christmas box. Don't be angry
with me! Don't take revenge. I'll give you all my rings...

(SCENE III; PP 209-210)

The Black Glove
(SVARTA HANDSKEN)

AUGUST STRINDBERG 1907
translated by Eivor Martinus 1991

The selfish **Young Wife** has accused her maid Ellen of stealing a
blue-stoned ring. The Christmas Spirit and Christmas Fairy of the
apartment block where she lives have been playing tricks on her to
make her benevolent at this festive time of year. They take a black
glove; they confuse her by interfering with the electricity and
plumbing. They also take her young daughter away to teach the
Young Wife remorse. Her child has been missing for two days now
and she is beside herself with grief.

> *The nursery. On the table two lit candles in silver candlesticks
> flanking a portrait of a child with flowers; a mirror is placed behind
> the candles, so the flames are reflected in the mirror. A child's white
> cot with a blue canopy.A doll sits on the chair: presents and a small
> Christmas tree are placed on the table. A white rocking horse beside
> the bed.*

YOUNG WIFE

Where is my child? Where are you, answer me.
Have you gone to the stars to play with other children,
not yet born, maybe dead and reborn?
Have you gone to seek the fairy tales
and meet Tom Thumb, Blue Bird
The Red Riding Hood and little Soliman,
when you got tired of us and our squabbles?
I wish I could come with you! I never felt at home here.
It held out promises that it didn't live up to...
It resembled, but was not...
a work of art perhaps, but badly flawed,
too much body and too little soul,
and how tragic that one could not be...
could not become what one most wanted to be.

(pause)

But it's dark. They have cut off the light...
(turns a light switch in vain)
And it's cold, they begrudge me heating.
(stretches out her hand as if looking for a tap)
 And no water. My flowers are thirsty.
(she rings a little bell)
But no one comes. Everyone has gone away.

Was I so bad? No one knows
what everyone knows ... they think they know.
Everyone was fawning on me and no one dared
tell me how I ought to be.
Yes, the mirror did, but it wasn't a good friend.
Its smooth glass only uttered politenesses.
(pause)

What's this? My lost glove.
And here, inside the finger is my ring!
Then she wasn't guilty after all, poor Ellen.
Now she'll take revenge, she'll punish me,
and the end will be worse than the beginning.
To prison? I don't want that ... I'll hide the ring.
(pause)

No! Yes! What was that? Someone stroked my cheek.
Is someone there? I heard someone whispering.
A child breathing in her sleep.
And now ... it's the weathercock on the neighbour's roof.
Shhh, he's singing on top of the chimney...
What does he say: "My Mary, Mary, Mary!"
And then: "Ellen, Ellen". Poor Ellen!"
A bell is ringing. The ambulance!
What's happened here? What have I done?
No, fair is fair, when I've done something wrong
I must go and take my punishment.

(SCENE V; PP 223-224

After the Fire
(Brända Tomten)

August Strindberg 1907
translated by Eivor Martinus 1991

The **Bricklayer's Wife** is quite a gossip. So when the ironmonger Valström's house is gutted by fire, she is delighted to find herself in her element as a nosey neighbour.

WIFE

That's funny, that means someone must have closed all the doors and taken the keys out before the fire started. That's strange!

(pause)

I used to work for the Valströms forty years ago, I know the family well, both the ironmonger and his brother who went to America, but I've heard that he's come back; the father was a good sort but the boys ... rather so-so. Mrs Vesterlund looked after that Rudolf, they never got on, you know, those brothers, always fighting and squabbling. I've seen a thing or two ... A lot of things have passed in this house, probably about time it was smoked out. Oh dear, what a house. They came and went, one after the other ... but they all came back here to die in the end ... they were born here, they got married here and they were divorced here. And the brother Arvid, the one that went to America, was thought to be dead for many years ... anyway ... he didn't claim his inheritance, but now they say he's back again ... but no one has seen him, of course ... there's so much talk. Look here is Valström back from the police station.

(Scene i; p 66)

The Mountain Giants
(I GIGANTI DELLA MONTAGNA)

LUIGI PIRANDELLO 1936
new version by Charles Wood 1993

La Sgricia is one of the old variety artists stranded in the Villa
Scalonga, where they all live a life of fantasy ('don't try to apply
reason. It's the way we live'). Each have their speciality act – hers is
the tale of how she died.

LA SGRICIA

When I got on the donkey I looked up and I knew it wasn't
morning but when you're a poor old woman what can you
do? He was giving me the lend of his donkey ... and if he
thought it was morning ... ? So I crossed myself, naturally,
and set off...

Under the stars, under the moon ... that's why he thought it
was morning, the moon ... such shadows, deep shadows ...
awful shadows and from the road the land slipped away ...
and so quiet, even the donkey's hooves muffled by the dust,
a long white road stretching for ever and me with my shawl
pulled down over my head for them shadows ... I must have
nodded off but I woke, in the middle of soldiers.

I felt much better thank you very much, troopers on big
horses on each side of me, led by a Captain on a white
horse, lovely animal. Thank God I thought, I'm safe now,
shadows or no ... thank you very much God I said but, no
sound, not a wink or a laugh from these young chaps none
of them more than twenty and I must have been a strange
sight – an old woman on a donkey in the middle of the
night. And no dust from their horses hooves, I made dust,
they didn't, or sound ... why? Yes. All the way to the
village. At Favara they halt, stand the way they do, soldiers,

daybreak shining through them, the Captain on his great white stallion, shoulders, legs, waiting for me on my little donkey, moon gone, flags flapping without a sound. *(she booms)* "Sgricia! I am the Hangel of the Century of God and these what have excorted you through the shadows of the moon and night is souls in Purgatory and as soon as you enter the village make your peace with God for you will DIE before noon!" Yes. That's right.

...My sister saw me. "What's up?" she said. "Get me a priest" I said. "What's wrong?" she said. "I'm going to die before twelve-o-clock" I said....*(she opens her arms)*...Do you think you're alive?

(La Sgricia has a finger up in front of Ilse, she slowly wags it.)

(ACT II; PP 46-47)

Figaro Gets Divorced
(FIGARO LÄSST SICH SCHEIDEN)

ÖDÖN VON HORVATH 1937
translated by Ian Huish 1990

Susanne and her husband Figaro have fled the revolution with their masters, the Almavivas. Falling into penury abroad, they leave the Almavivas to set up a hairdressing salon in Grosshadersdorf (Figaro was once, of course, the Barber of Seville). Susanne detests having to grovel to the *petit bourgeois* customers and is saddened that she has grown apart from Figaro. She has always wanted a child, but Figaro has always resisted. With the encouragement of a midwife customer, she pretends that she is pregnant. Figaro thinks it is 'a disaster'. A row ensues.

SUSANNE

I don't want your baby any more – And if I did have one I'd crawl away and hide like a bitch so that you wouldn't even know where your child had first seen the light of day, so that he wouldn't be cursed by you, since you don't even want him to live – I'd never let you see your child, never! You don't deserve anything else, you're the Kiss of Death, d'you hear, Death!

Figaro, I lied to you just now. I'm not expecting your baby – I only said I was so you'd at least take pity on me. It was just a trick – Your wife wanted to trick you so that she might become a mother through you, you, her lord and master. But it's all over now. The man she wanted to have a child by doesn't live in Grosshadersdorf. I dreamt about him last night. He leaned over me and his shadow was three times the size of the earth. I could see him so clearly. My one true love.

He's dead. He was called Figaro.

Yes, my Figaro looked forward to the future when there
was a thunderstorm and he leapt to the window when the
lightning struck, but you? You won't even leave the house
without an umbrella! My Figaro went to prison because he
wrote what he believed, you wouldn't even dare to read in
secret the things that he wrote! My Figaro would be the first
to confront Count Almaviva with the truth, at the height of
his powers, you just keep up appearances in
Grosshadersdorf! You are a narrow-minded petty bourgeois,
he was a citizen of the world. He was a man and you –

Once you used to know but now you've forgotten
everything.

(ACT II, SCENE III; PP 126-128)

Bibliography

Three books which helpfully put the European classic repertoire into a modern theatre context are:
99 Play: Key Plays Since The Orestia
    Nicholas Wright, Methuen, 1992
The Citz: 21 Years of the Glasgow Citizens Theatre
    Michael Coveney, Nick Hern Books, 1990
Cheek by Jowl: Ten Years of Celebration
    Simon Reade, Absulute Classics, 1991

Although it deals exclusively with Shakespeare characters, the best insight into women's classical roles comes in:
Clamorous Voices, Carol Rutter, Women's Press, 1988

The translated plays in the Absolute Monologues series are all published by Absolute Classics:
After the Fire, The Chamber Plays, Strindberg/Martinus 1991
Anatol, Schnitzler/Robinson, 1989
Bérénice, Three Plays, Racine/Bartlett, 1990
The Black Glove, The Chamber Plays, Strindberg/Martinus, 1991
Le Cid, Corneille Three Plays, Noel Clark, 1993
Don't Fool with Love, de Musset Three Plays, Donnellan, 1993
A Door must be Kept Open or Shut, de Musset Three Plays, Donnellan, 1993
A Family Affrair, Ostrovsky/Dear, 1989
Figaro Gets Divorced, Horváth Two Plays, Huish, 1991
Fuente Ovejuna, Lope de Vega Two Plays, Mitchell, 1989
The Game of Love and Chance, Marivaux/Bartlett, 1992
The Gentleman from Olmedo, Lope de Vega Two Plays, Johnston, 1992
Hecuba, Euripides/McLeish, 1995

The Illusion, Corneille Two Plays, Bolt, 1989

The Last Days of Don Juan, Tirso de Molina/Dear, 1990

Life's a Dream, Calderón Three Plays, Mitchell & Barton, 1990

Lost in a Mirror, Lope de Vega Two Plays, Mitchell, 1989

The Mayor of Zalamea, Calderón Three Plays, Mitchell, 1990

Mirandolina, Goldoni Two Plays, Bolt, 1993

Le Misanthrope, Three Plays, Molière/Bartlett, 1990

The Mountain Giants, Pirandello/Wood, 1993

Orestes, Euripides/McLeish, 1995

The Pelican, The Chamber Plays, Strindberg/Martinus, 1991

Polyeuct, Corneille Three Plays, Noel Clark, 1993

The Power of Darkness, Tolstoy/Anthony Clark, 1989

The Real Don Juan, Zorrilla/Bolt, 1990

Rosmersholm, Ibsen Two Plays, Rudkin, 1990

Sara, Lessing Two Plays, Bell, 1990

The School for Wives, Three Plays, Molière/Bartlett, 1990

The Sisterhood, Molière Two Plays, Bolt, 1991

Successful Strategies, Marivaux Three Plays, Wertenbaker, 1989

Thérèse Raquin, Zola/Broughton, 1989

Thunder in the Air, Strindberg/Martinus, 1989

Thunder in the Air, The Chamber Plays, Strindberg/Martinus, 1991

Virgins Vows, Fredro Three Plays, Noel Clark, 1993

Women of Troy, Euripides/McLeish, 1995

ABSOLUTE CLASSICS titles can be ordered direct from the publisher: 14 Widcombe Cresent, Bath, BA2 6AH, England. Tel 0225 316013 Fax 0225 445836